Cape FLAVOUR

FOR VERN – WITH LOVE

MYRNA ROBINS

PICTURE CREDITS

AJ = Anthony Johnson, AP/STB = Alain Proust/Steenberg, BF = courtesy of Bouchard Finlayson, BC = courtesy of Bon Courage, BKH = courtesy of Boekenhoutskloof, BRN = courtesy of Branewynsdraai, CC = courtesy of Citrusdal Cellars, CVD = Charley von Dugteren, DH = courtesy of Durbanville Hills, DMS = courtesy of Diemersfontein, DOW = courtesy of De Oude Welgemoed, DS/PA = D Steele/Photo Access, ET = Erhardt Thiel, G/DR/PA = Getaway/David Rogers/ Photo Access, G/PW/PA = Getaway/Patrick Wagner/Photo Access, G/CL/PA = Getaway/C Lanz/Photo Access, GP = courtesy of Groote Post, GR = courtesy of Grand Roche, HC = Haute Cabriere, HPH/PA = HPH Photography/Photo Access, HR = courtesy of Hamilton Russell, HVH = Hein von Horsten, JB/LQF = Jeremy Browne/Le Quartier Francais, JS = courtesy of Jessica's, KY/PA = Keith Young/ Photo Access, LK/PR = photographer Leon Kriel, courtesy of Poplars Restaurant, LVH/PA = Lanz von Horsten/Photo Access, MDV = courtesy of Middlevlei, MR = courtesy of Mons Ruber, MS = Mark Skinner, MSB = courtesy of Muisbosskerm, PH/LPF = Paddy Howes/La Petite Ferme, PON = courtesy of Pontac, PP = Peter Pickford, R = Ryno, RBK = courtesy of Rhebokskloof, RC = courtesy of River Cafe, SA = Shaen Adey, SAT = courtesy of www.southafrica-travel.net, SIL = Struik Image Library, SP = courtesy of Spier, TM = courtesy of The Marine, VER = courtesy of Vergelegen, VR = courtesy of Van Ryn, WFD = courtesy of Waterford, WK = Walter Knirr, WR = courtesy 96 Winery Road

All food photography © Neil Corder/Struik Image Library
All map illustrations © Sean Robertson/Struik Image Library

Front cover: top left and bottom right: SA/SIL; top right: R/SIL; Back cover: top left: PH/LPF; top right: WK/SIL; bottom: SA/SIL; Inside back flap: SA/SIL; P 2-3: SA/SIL; P 5: top & bottom: SA/SIL; P 6: (3) WFD, (6): LK/PR, (8) R/SIL; P 10: (1-4) & bottom left SA/SIL, (5) RC, (6) ET/SIL; P 11: AJ/SIL; P 13: AP/STB; P 14: SA/SIL; P 18: (1& 3) DH, (2) SA/SIL, (4&5) LK/PR, (6) DOW; P 19: SA/SIL; P 20/21: DH; P 23: DOW; P 28: (1) SP, (2,3,4,5 & 6) & bottom right above, bottom left SA/SIL, bottom right: WFD; P 29: SA/SIL; P 30: WFD; P 34: SA/SIL; P 36: MDV; P 37: KY/PA; P 46: (1) WK/SIL, (2) SA/SIL, (3&4) VER, (5) WR; P 47: SA/SIL; P 54: (1) ET/SIL, (2,4 & 6) SA/SIL, (3) GR, (5) PON, (7) MS/SIL; P 55: SA/SIL; P 56/57: RBK; P 58: GR; P 61: HVH; P 62: DMS; P 70: (1, 4 & 6) SA/SIL, (2 & 5) JB/LQF, (3) PH/LPF, above bottom right: BKH; P 71: SA/SIL; P 72/73: HC; P 75: SA/SIL; P 76: JB/LQF; P 77: top PH/LPF, bottom SA/SIL; P 86: (1) LVH, (2 & 4) SA/SIL, (3) R/SIL; P 87: HR; P 88/89: LVH/BF; P 91: TM; P 92: LVH; P 93: WK/SIL; P 98: (1, 3, 4 & bottom left) SA/SIL, (2) HVH/SIL; P 99: SA/SIL; P 100: SA/SIL, (2) CVD; P 104: CVD; P 105: VR; P 110: (1, 2 & 5) SA/SIL, (3 & 6) BC, (4) BRN; P 111: SA/SIL, P 113: SAT; P 114/115: SA/SIL; P 116: LVH; P 117: BRN; P 124: (1) SA/SIL, (2) G/DR/PA, (3) G/PW/PA, (4) G/LZ/PA; P 125: HPH/PA; P 126/127: LVH/PA; P 129: JS; P 130: MR; P 131: SA/SIL; P 136: (1, 2, 3, 4 & 5) SA/SIL, above bottom centre: PP/SIL; P 137: SA/SIL; P 138-139: KY/PA; P 141: GP; P 143: DS/PA; P 148: CC; P 149: CVD/SIL; P 151: MSB; P 152: SA/SIL

Struik Publishers
(a division of New Holland Publishing (Pty) Ltd)
Cornelis Struik House, 80 McKenzie Street
Cape Town 8001

New Holland Publishing is a member of the
Johnnic Publishing Group

First published in 2003

1 2 3 4 5 6 7 8 9 10

PUBLISHING MANAGER: Linda de Villiers
EDITOR: Pat Barton
CONCEPT DESIGN: Petal Palmer
DESIGNER: Beverley Dodd
STYLIST: Abigail Donnelly
PROOFREADER AND INDEXER: Sean Fraser

Reproduction by Hirt & Carter (Cape) (Pty) Ltd
Printed and bound by Kyodo

ISBN 1 86872 841 2

Log on to our photographic website
www.imagesofafrica.co.za for an African experience.

The Publisher wishes to thank @home, Boardmans,
Nocturnal Affair, Summer House, The Yellow Door
and Woolworths for the generous loan of props used
in the food photography.

www.struik.co.za

C ONTENTS

INTRODUCTION 7

CONSTANTIA 11

DURBANVILLE 19

STELLENBOSCH 29

HELDERBERG 47

PAARL AND WELLINGTON 55

FRANSCHHOEK 71

OVERBERG 87

WORCESTER 99

ROBERTSON 111

LITTLE KAROO 125

SWARTLAND 137

OLIFANTS RIVER 149

FOOD AND WINE FESTIVALS 157

INDEX 159

INTRODUCTION

For the adventurous gourmet, wine connoisseur and traveller who relishes unearthing regional and traditional specialities, the Western Cape is a gastronomic mecca, harbouring a feast of flavours and a wealth of wonderful wines.

ABOVE *Margie's tomato and brinjal tart.*

OPPOSITE *Chicken salad with fruit and nuts (1); Duo of yellowtail and tiger prawns (2); Waterford winery (3); Smoked salmon on blinis (4); Lamb knuckle with dried fruit (5); Poplars Restaurant (6); Decadent chocolate cake (7); Walker Bay Wines (8).*

From the southernmost tip of Africa to its northern boundary in the harsh uplands of the Karoo, from the green hills edging the Indian Ocean in the east to the windswept shores of the Atlantic in the west, the Western Cape province encompasses 130 000 sq kilometres of astonishing diversity and extraordinary beauty.

Along with vivid contrasts in scenery, climate, flora and fauna, visitors will encounter a wide variety in local food and wine styles during journeys through regions as spectacular as they are dissimilar.

Some three and a half centuries have passed since the first vegetable garden was planted at the foot of Table Mountain. Vine cuttings took root alongside a year or two later, and the first wine was produced in the late summer of 1659.

By then Cape cuisine was starting to evolve as the *veldkos* and local seafood enjoyed by the indigenous Bushman and Khoi population were incorporated into the diet of the Dutch settlers.

From the close of the 17th century, mercenaries, political exiles and slaves from the Orient brought with them exotic spices and the culinary know-how that were to transform bland local fare into the spicy and distinctive cuisine we savour today.

French, German, British and Portuguese influences have added to the flavourful mix over the centuries, while contemporary Cape cooks follow global trends with the same enthusiasm as their counterparts in kitchens worldwide.

Outdoor cooking is part of the national ethos, characterised by both the braai or barbecue and potjiekos. The latter involves stews simmering in a three-legged cast-iron pot over a small fire and was the staple culinary technique of early trekboers and transport riders. This pioneer cookery was revived in the 1970s.

The resurgence and expansion of the Cape wine industry since 1990 have been accompanied by a boom in exports and welcome interchange of ideas with wine-producing countries across the world. This has contributed to the production of many superior – and some sensational – Cape wines, which are garnering rave reviews from across the globe.

Dining and wining at the Cape can be relaxed or formal, simple or exotic: Whether your taste leans toward rock lobster teamed with a top-of-the-range chardonnay or potjiekos partnered by a robust red blend, you will find plenty to savour as you meander along the highways and byways of the Western Cape's distinctive regions.

From a total approaching 400 cellars – estates, co-operatives, boutique and *garagiste* wineries – a representative selection has been listed, while restaurants included range from guesthouse dining rooms to five-star venues, from seaside bomas to farmhouse kitchens.

Along with safe journeys, memorable meals and exciting wines, I hope that in your pairing of Cape fare with our wines, you create gastronomic synergies both unique and memorable.

Only cellars which are open to the public for tasting and sales without prior appointment have been included. This has meant that one or two important wineries – such as Meerlust in Stellenbosch and Morgenster in Somerset West – have been omitted.

In view of the many sponsored publications appearing today, I would like to emphasise that no owner, winemaker, chef or restaurateur paid for their establishment to be included in this book – in fact only those who were approached for recipes knew of its existence.

I am indebted to these generous contributors for their special recipes, which, whether traditional or

contemporary, are touched by the flavour of the Cape. My grateful thanks also go to Felicity Rennie of Vignerons de Franschhoek, Genevieve Faure of the Helderberg Wine Route and Peggy Lannon, formerly of Paarl Vintners, for their willing help and invaluable information.

MYRNA ROBINS
Blouberg
February 2003

1. Bonnievale	10. Lutzville
2. Cape Town CBD	11. Paarl
3. Constantia	12. Porterville
4. Darling	13. Robertson
5. De Rust	14. Somerset West
6. Durbanville	15. Stellenbosch
7. Elgin	16. Tulbagh
8. Franschhoek	17. Wellington
9. Hermanus	18. Worcester

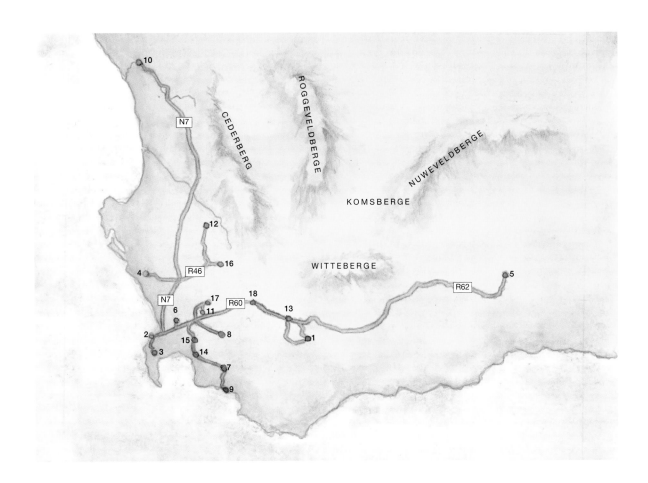

NTRODUCTION

It is more than appropriate that we start our gastronomic journey in the region where the first quality wines were produced at the Cape, some 320 years ago. To complement them, early hosts kept a fine table, another tradition that endures in this fair valley. Not only do the winelands share expensive space with one of Cape Town's top suburbs, but Constantia can also lay claim to being the oldest wine region in the New World.

CONSTANTIA

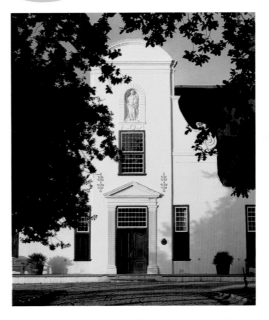

ABOVE *Groot Constantia manor house.*

OPPOSITE *Klein Constantia (1); Jonkershuis restaurant (2); Pontac grapes (3); Buitenverwachting (4); Spaanschemat River Café (5); Groot Constantia cellar museum (6).*

Its wine route has been dubbed the Big Five – but instead of wildlife, visitors will encounter a series of magnificent historic farms, strung like a jewelled necklace along the slopes of the Constantiaberg.

The name 'Constantia' is irrevocably linked with the superb sweet wine produced there in the 18th and 19th centuries which was lauded by European royalty and British aristocracy. Subsequent decades saw wine production taking a back seat, and it was only in the last quarter of the 20th century that a remarkable renaissance occurred: the restoration of surviving architectural gems, accompanied by a revival of the production of world-class wines.

History, beauty, winning wines and fine fare make an enviable package of attractions. However, Constantia boasts two further advantages for visitors: the valley is a mere 20-minute drive from the centre of Cape Town, and the compact wine route means that even those with limited time can fit all five farms into their schedule.

But we recommend that visitors take a leaf or two out of the books of early travellers … follow in the footsteps of those visitors from more leisurely eras, who called at Constantia estates, assured of gracious hospitality, fine wines and tables laden with good food. We know that you will savour a similar experience.

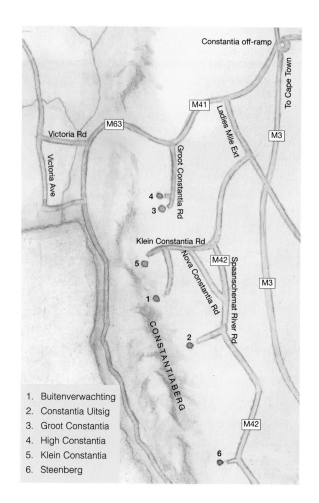

1. Buitenverwachting
2. Constantia Uitsig
3. Groot Constantia
4. High Constantia
5. Klein Constantia
6. Steenberg

DELICIOUS FRUIT OF THE VINE

In late summer, during the mellow month of March, it's time to gorge on the valley's luscious, honey-sweet hanepoot (Muscat d'Alexandrie) grapes; three-stalked bunches of berries browned by the hot southern sun.

Constantia farmstalls can hardly keep up with the demand, while nimble hawkers skip between lanes of traffic to offer trays of grapes to motorists waiting at traffic lights and stop streets.

It's a Cape tradition to preserve these golden orbs in a brandied syrup. After maturing for at least three months, Kaapsche Jongens, as the grapes are called, add spirited sweetness to winter social occasions (recipe on page 106).

Heritage cooks prefer hanepoot grapes when making *korrelkonfyt* (grape jam), delicious on wholewheat bread and a time-honoured accompaniment to braaied snoek.

Indulge your palate in the Constantia winelands

Locals are spoilt for choice when dining out, with restaurants in shopping centres and popular pubs vying with gourmet venues.

The wine farms are home to many of the best restaurants; only two of the valley wineries do not also boast a restaurant.

As if to make up for that, most of the others have more than one, and it is serendipitous that the menus of these restaurants embrace a blend of traditional and contemporary temptations that well illustrate the diversity of Cape cuisine. The wide variety of estate wines makes the matching of food to wine a delightful task.

The cool maritime climate of the Constantiaberg slopes creates near-perfect conditions for wine grapes and − in addition − one can only reflect that, of all possible beautiful settings, the late 17th-century Cape Governor Simon van der Stel surely chose the loveliest for his home and vineyards.

Visiting **Groot Constantia** is as much a journey back in time as it is about tasting wine and heritage fare. The oak-fringed complex of manor house (now a cultural museum that reflects the era of Hendrik Cloete), the exquisite old wine cellar named after Cloete, and the buildings on the west side of the forecourt all offer a striking contrast to the modern production cellar. After your cellar tour, be sure to taste both the range of

Steenberg, the most southerly and oldest of the great wine farms of Constantia, in its new role as luxury country hotel.

Buitenverwachting was well named by its 18th-century owner who found the beauty of its setting 'beyond expectation'.

white wines and the flagship red blend known as the Gouverneurs Reserve.

Back in the **Jonkershuis**, built in 1800 to house the expanding Cloete family, the Watrobski family have been dispensing bountiful breakfasts, teas and lunches for more than 20 years. Contemporary fare is on the menu, but this is the perfect venue to indulge in Cape heritage specialities such as *smoorsnoek*, *bobotie*, sweet potatoes in orange sauce, and brandy pud. Order a Cape sampler for a melange of nostalgic tastes. The restaurant below the production cellar makes a cosmopolitan alternative.

Right next door, the boutique winery of **High Constantia** presents a striking contrast to the imposing cellars that surround it. Dodge the chickens as you head for the garden cellar, where Chardonnay, Cabernet Sauvignon and Cabernet Franc mature in oak barrels. Do not miss the flagship blend, Sebastiaan, named after a 19th-century owner and vintner of this former estate.

Less than a century after Simon van der Stel started producing red wine at Groot Constantia, Hendrik Cloete was producing the sweet wine that was to make Constantia a household name among the aristocracy of Europe and the British Isles.

The grapes for this sought-after dessert wine were grown on **Klein Constantia**, a subdivision of the original estate. Today the restored Cape Dutch farmstead is complemented by a beautiful winery, with modern vaulted-barrel maturation cellars. While noted for its brilliant Sauvignon Blanc and noble reds, it is the re-creation of the legendary Constantia wine, the prestigious Vin de Constance – made from raisined Muscat de Frontignan – that catapulted this estate onto the global wine map.

Deep in the valley, off the Klein Constantia Road, a circular route passes paddocks and vineyards en route to the cellars and restaurants of **Buitenverwachting**. The lawned court, which today accommodates

picnickers, is lined by the gracious manor house and original outbuildings, which date from the late 18th century. The farm's fortunes rose and fell over the years, but the estate was in a decline when the Mueller family purchased it, restored the old buildings, built new facilities and planted selected cultivars.

Today Buitenverwachting is equally renowned for its wine, its cuisine and its sound environmental practices.

Perfectionist winemaker Hermann Kirschbaum consistently produces superb whites: Sauvignon Blanc, Chardonnay, Rhine Riesling and the popular Buiten Blanc. Red-wine production is increasing, and the Pinot Noir, Cabernet, Merlot and Christine (a claret blend), should also be sampled.

During the warmer months, visitors can order an elegant picnic, or savour continental fare on the terrace of the informal **Café Petite**. But gourmets from across the globe head for the formal **Buitenverwachting Restaurant**, a venue that is consistently rated among the top 10 in the country.

Decision-making is difficult, as diners are tempted with a table d'hôte and an à la carte menu, both of which change daily. Then there are the vegetarian and the Mediterranean menus, the crayfish and the venison cartes and – for connoisseurs with staying power – a glorious menu dégustation. Whatever you eventually choose, your selection will be perfectly cooked, artistically plated and professionally served.

The entrance to **Constantia Uitsig** is easy to find when you are travelling towards Tokai along the Spaanschemat River Road. This farm and small hotel are renowned more for fine fare than for their wines.

This is because wine production started comparatively recently, but already Uitsig Chardonnay has garnered a clutch of awards.

For informal feasts, the **Spaanschemat River Café** (see page 17) is unsurpassed. At peak season it is not uncommon to see cars and 4x4s lined up waiting for the doors to open, so occupants can start their day with Eggs Benedict on the lavender-fringed terrace. Partners Judy Badenhorst and Graham Isaacson combine talents to present chic, irresistible country fare.

The original **Uitsig** restaurant, housed in the farmstead, presents a Mediterranean mix, with popular pastas, Florentine tripe and wild duck with polenta among the specialities.

Then there's **La Colombe**, where passionate chef Franck Dangereux titillates the palate with brilliant renderings of Provençal fare that transport diners from this poolside venue to the south of France. His sauces are worth dieting for.

The last, and most southerly, of the Big Five original Constantia homes is **Steenberg**, a vast estate that now includes a golf course and up-market residences.

The modern winery sits among the vineyards on the slopes of the 'stone mountain', where visitors enjoy panoramic views along with award-winning Sauvignon Blancs and aromatic Semillons. The estate has already proved its potential for red-wine production, notably with its Merlot.

The historic heart of the farm is the court enclosed by the gabled manor house, now a boutique hotel, and the original wine cellar, now housing a welcoming restaurant that serves cosmopolitan fare – with a nod to the Cape and a bow to the Orient.

Visitors taking the scenic route to the southern tip of the Cape Peninsula will see vines on the slopes of Red Hill and the Noordhoek mountains. The wines produced from these maritime vineyards are the products of the recently established ward of Cape Point.

JONKERSHUIS SMOORSNOEK

This classic Cape Malay dish is a perennial favourite among upcountry visitors, as well as those from overseas. Helen Watrobski gets her snoek from Hout Bay, where it is oak-smoked the traditional way.

1 kg smoked snoek, weighed after skinning
   and filleting
60 ml (4 tbsp) butter
60 ml (4 tbsp) oil
1 fresh green chilli, finely minced
2 large onions, peeled and finely chopped
2 large potatoes, peeled, diced and parboiled
2 tomatoes, skinned and chopped (optional)
salt and milled black pepper
30 ml (2 tbsp) mild fruit chutney

Flake the snoek, removing any small bones.

Heat the butter and oil together in large, deep frying pan, add the chilli and onions and sauté until golden. Add the drained parboiled potatoes and turn in the butter mixture until well coated. Add the flaked snoek, stirring gently so that the ingredients do not get mashed.

Add the tomatoes, if using, then cover the frying pan and steam the mixture gently for about 5 minutes.

Just before serving, taste to see if salt is needed, and grind over black pepper to taste. Gently stir in the chutney.

Serve with sweet potatoes baked in orange juice, white rice and a green vegetable, if wanted. Offer a bowl of *korrelkonfyt* (grape jam with pips) separately.

Serves 6

SPAANSCHEMAT RIVER CAFÉ PRAWN
AND GRAPEFRUIT SALAD WITH MANGO DRESSING

24 king prawns, thawed if frozen

MARINADE
juice and grated zest of 1 lemon
1 clove garlic, finely chopped
1 handful fresh coriander, coarsely chopped
pinch salt
black pepper

SALAD
300 g baby green beans, trimmed
30 fresh asparagus spears, trimmed
125 g mangetout
1 English cucumber
4 pillow packs watercress
2 pink grapefruit, halved and segments removed

DRESSING OR SALSA
30 ml (2 tbsp) lemon juice
250 ml (1 cup) sunflower oil
10 ml (2 tsp) fish sauce
juice and grated zest of 3 limes
1 large mango, peeled and stoned
1 clove garlic
2.5 cm piece of fresh ginger, peeled and finely grated
1 medium hot red chilli, finely chopped
250 ml (1 cup) fresh coriander leaves
125 ml (½ cup) mint leaves

GARNISH
extra coriander leaves

Remove the heads of the prawns, then devein and peel the tails, leaving on the last tail segment. Combine the marinade ingredients and toss with the prawns. Chill, covered, for at least 2 hours.

Blanch the beans, asparagus and mangetout separately in boiling water for 3–5 minutes each, leaving the saucepan uncovered. Refresh in ice-cold water. Drain well. Peel long ribbons from the cucumber, using a vegetable peeler, and place them in ice-cold water. Wash and dry the watercress.

Grill the prawns in a heated grilling pan for about 2½ minutes on each side, or until pink and opaque. Cool.

Place the dressing ingredients in a food processor or blender, in the order listed, and blend for 2 minutes. Adjust the seasoning.. For a salsa rather than a dressing, dice the mango and combine it with the blended ingredients.

To serve, arrange the watercress on a large platter or individual plates. Arrange the mangetout, asparagus, beans and grapefruit segments over the watercress. Top with the prawns and drizzle the mango dressing (or spoon the salsa) over. Add the well-drained cucumber ribbons and scatter extra fresh coriander over the salad.

Serves 6 as a starter or 4 as a main course

DURBANVILLE

Durbanville, founded in the 19th century

as an outspan for farmers heading for

Cape Town, was originally called

Pampoenskraal, a name that has been

perpetuated in an open-air restaurant

on Altydgedacht farm.

ABOVE *The old bell tower at Altydgedacht.*

OPPOSITE *@ the Hills (1); Altydgedacht (2); Durbanville Hills (3); Poplars (4 & 5); Frans de Wet and David Grier of De Oude Welgemoed (6).*

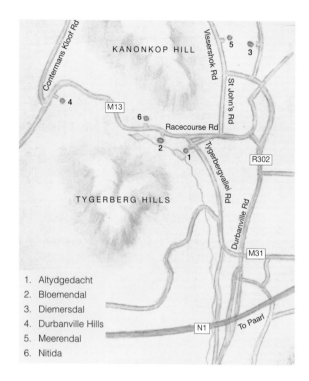

1. Altydgedacht
2. Bloemendal
3. Diemersdal
4. Durbanville Hills
5. Meerendal
6. Nitida

There is, however, nothing rustic about some of the fine vintages – on sale at pleasing prices – that emanate from the cellars.

Four of the farms within this ward celebrated their tercentenary recently. They were established soon after officials from the newly built castle at the Cape of Good Hope were sent out, in about 1656, to map the 'tiger' hills and to hunt for meat. These early cattle farmers diversified as the years rolled by, inspiring the 18th-century German traveller Peter Kolb to describe their

The wine farms of Durbanville are not as well known as those in larger – and trendier – wards and districts. This adds immeasurably to their charm, particularly for the independent traveller seeking to avoid crowds.

All but one of the six farms that constitute an informal route through the 'spotted hills' of the Tygerberg (literally, tiger or leopard mountain) are venues that have simple tasting facilities, and all are manned by hospitable staff happy to introduce their products.

Given that the oldest farms are mere minutes from one of the largest shopping centres in the country, it is remarkable that they have survived at all, and that they retain their air of rustic simplicity.

farms thus: 'In the cornfields, vineyards and gardens … nature appears methinks, in all her pride and luxury … she distributes her bounty with a very lavish hand.'

This still holds true, with nature providing a backdrop of verdant beauty to vinous explorations. It is also in keeping that the best restaurants of the region are housed in former farmsteads, venues in which to relish generous servings of country fare that remains in touch with its Cape roots. Durbanville wines well complement gastronomic treats in these surroundings.

PRODUCE FROM TOWN AND COUNTRY

The historic core of Durbanville retains well-maintained links with the past, and an open-air market still stocks local farm cheese and yoghurt, along with seasonal fruit and vegetables. The Homecraft Centre tantalizes with an irresistible selection of home bakes, sweet and

The ultra-modern Durbanville Hills winery boasts a commanding position and panoramic views.

savoury, including old-fashioned Afrikaner favourites such as *koeksisters*, *gemmerkoekies* (ginger biscuits) and *mosbolletjies* that are hard to find today.

Orchards of old and gnarled fig trees on historic farms still yield sweet summer fruits, which are transformed into preserves, and local cooks make good use of seafood harvested from the Atlantic Ocean, just a sea breeze away.

THE WINE FARMS OF DURBANVILLE
Heading north from the Tygervalley shopping complex, you will swop noise and traffic fumes for the tranquil surrounds of **Altydgedacht**, one of the Cape's oldest wine farms and the first to be registered (in 1698) in the area known as the 'leopard mountain'. The farm was originally named Tygerberg, and wine has been sold from this estate since 1730.

Among the many fascinating stories that make up the farm's history are those of successive women of wine who made significant contributions over the centuries.

Today John and Oliver Parker, the talented and unassuming fifth-generation owners, get on with the job of producing award-winning red wines – including a Barbera, the only place in the Cape you will find wine made from this Italian grape. But try the whites as well, especially the Sauvignon Blanc and Gewürztraminer.

Neighbouring **Bloemendal** benefits from the energy and passion of proprietor and winemaker Jackie Coetzee. Encouraged by the Parkers, he made his first wines in the 1980s; today a range of reds, including an excellent Shiraz, emanate from revamped cellars and his Sauvignon Blanc offers further proof that Durbanville is a great region for this cultivar.

Over the hill – literally but certainly not figuratively – lies **Diemersdal** estate, owned by the Louw family for more than a century. Another farm that has celebrated its tercentenary, Diemersdal is also renowned for quality red wines that have been exported for decades. Today, South Africans can also enjoy the highly rated Cabernet Sauvignon and Shiraz and sample their promising red blend.

The historical quartet is completed with **Meerendal**, a farm that boasted 60 000 vines way back in 1712. Today, sensibly priced reds are their forte.

Heading westwards along Racecourse Road, travellers need to keep an eye open for the sign indicating the entrance to **Nitida**, a recently established boutique cellar that houses a treasury of exciting wines. Bernhard and Peta Veller exchanged high-powered careers for farming and winemaking, and their hard work has been rewarded with significant success. Reds and whites alike are commanding attention and garnering awards; try the Chardonnay and the Sauvignon Blanc, and don't overlook the claret-style red blend, Calligraphy.

'Big and bold' describes both newcomer cellar **Durbanville Hills** and its enthusiastic and genial winemaker, Martin Moore. The winery is housed in an ultra-modern cellar, built from stone, slate and glass, where all of the Cape's so-called Big Six are made.

High volumes on the one hand contrast with limited releases in the Rhinofields and Single Vineyard range on the other. All the reds are rated highly and Moore has also proved his assertion that Durbanville is Sauvignon Blanc country.

It was here, in 2002, at a function to mark the visit to the Cape by wine writers from several countries, that more than one North American fundi pronounced the region's Sauvignon Blancs to be as good as those produced anywhere else in the world, which has resulted in ripples of trans-Atlantic interest.

Sea breezes from the chilly Atlantic reduce summer temperatures and aerate the vineyards in the undulating hills of the Tygerberg, contributing to the high quality of Durbanville's wine grapes.

DINING OUT IN DURBANVILLE

Whether it's line fish from the West Coast or lamb from the farm, wines from the surrounding hills and dales complement local ingredients to perfection

At **De Oude Welgemoed**, an up-market restaurant, an informal bistro and a walk-in wine cellar share space in a historic farmhouse that is a mecca for local and upcountry food lovers.

Chef and restaurateur David Grier has established an enviable reputation for consistency and quality over two decades. His innovative fare is prettily plated but also comes in portions substantial enough to satisfy robust appetites. The excellent wine list attracts annual awards, and there is a cellar lined with rare and vintage wines for connoisseurs.

More recently, another venerable Durbanville farmstead opened its doors in a new role as **Poplars**, a multifaceted restaurant. The rambling building (which is reputed to have been one of Simon van der Stel's hunting lodges, and harbours an unidentified ghost) has undergone extensive restoration and alteration and the interior now sports a contemporary décor. The complex opened to almost instant acclaim, catering for everyone from gastronomes to families looking for weekend barbecues; from sophisticated party-goers to hikers arriving for al fresco breakfasts. Local farmers who equate dining out with large steaks are just as happy here as those who opt for Jacques Botha's trendier dishes. This is one of the few venues that come close to pleasing every palate and most purses.

The dramatic modern winery at Durbanville Hills also houses **@ the Hills**, a restaurant with heart-stopping views, that serves lunches every day. Seasonal, unpretentious cuisine is enhanced by the use of traditional West Coast ingredients, when available. Not only snoek, but also snoek roe and liver, sometimes find their way onto the menu over the weekend.

De Oude Welgemoed restaurant ready for its nightly influx of diners.

DE OUDE WELGEMOED'S MUSHROOM AND BLUE CHEESE MOUSSELINE

Chef David Grier is a talented, friendly and prolific chef whose innovative recipes are appreciated by legions of regular diners at De Oude Welgemoed. His efforts are also frequently recognized by competition judges. David was placed second in the SA Chef of the Year contest in 2001. This vegetarian dish makes a flavourful, easy-to-prepare starter.

olive oil
150 g white button mushrooms, sliced
150 g brown mushrooms, sliced
a few finely chopped fresh rosemary needles
salt and pepper
60 g blue cheese, grated

3 eggs
100 ml fresh cream
1 clove garlic, crushed
basil leaves
150 g oyster mushrooms
wholegrain mustard sauce (optional)

Oil a non-stick pan and heat it, then add the white and brown mushrooms and the rosemary and braise the mixture until the mushrooms are cooked. Season with salt and pepper.

Transfer the contents of the pan to a blender. Add the cheese, eggs and cream and blend until mixed but not smooth. Divide the mousse mixture among 6 greased tea cups and microwave on 100 per cent power for about 6 minutes.

Meanwhile, heat a little olive oil, add the garlic and a few basil leaves.

Add the oyster mushrooms and cook until just done.

Unmould the mushroom mousseline onto 6 flat plates and garnish with the oyster mushrooms.

The optional sauce is made by combining dry white wine, which has been reduced by half, with fresh cream, then stirring in wholegrain mixed mustard to taste. Heat until smooth, then drizzle around the mousselines.

Serves 6

BACON-WRAPPED SIRLOIN WITH BLACK MUSHROOMS AND A RED-WINE GLAZE

Jacques Botha is both a successful restaurateur and a talented chef, as the huge success of Poplar's restaurant attests. Although the menu caters for all tastes, there are many regulars who look no further than the recommended steak of the day when ordering.

8 sprigs fresh rosemary
4 x 250 g sirloin steaks, well aged
8 rashers rindless back bacon
sunflower or olive oil
4 large black mushrooms, wiped clean

2 cloves garlic, crushed
250 ml (1 cup) dry red wine
250 ml (1 cup) beef stock
salt and black pepper

Preheat the oven to 180 °C.
Place a rosemary sprig on each steak, then wrap the steaks in bacon rashers and secure them with a toothpick.
Set aside.
Heat a little oil in a large, deep frying pan, add the mushrooms and cook on both sides, turning carefully, until they are nearly tender. Add the crushed garlic halfway through and sauté, stirring, but do not let it brown.
Transfer the mushrooms and garlic to a plate.
Return the pan to the stove and add a little additional oil, if necessary. Fry the bacon-wrapped steaks quickly on both sides, then transfer them to an ovenproof dish and roast them for 10 minutes.
Meanwhile, pour the wine and the stock into the frying pan and bring to the boil, stirring often.
Cook until the sauce reduces and thickens, then check the seasoning. If necessary, thicken with a little cornflour mixed to a paste with a little water.
To serve, place a mushroom in the centre of each of 4 plates. Top with the sirloin steaks. Divide the wine glaze between the 4 steaks, pouring it carefully over them. Garnish with the remaining rosemary sprigs.

Serves 4

$STELLENBOSCH

Roads lead to Stellenbosch from every
point of the compass, cutting through
some of the country's most valuable
vineyards, en route to a town blessed
with an abundance of attractions.
This is an intoxicating region where the
historic and the contemporary share
a setting of incomparable beauty; where
a gallery of craggy mountains frames
valleys that produce some of the best
wine in the New World.

ABOVE   *Historic Lanzerac manor house.*

OPPOSITE   *The Spier estate (1); Restaurant (2);
pine avenue (3); and valley views on Neethlingshof
estate (6); Oude Nektar (4); Zevenwacht (5).*

The Eerste (literally, first) River winds its way through the intensely cultivated valley that is home to Stellenbosch. How different it must have been in 1679 when newly appointed Cape Governor Simon van der Stel crossed this, the first river he had encountered since leaving Cape Town.

Impressed by the potential of his surroundings, he decided to make land grants to settlers along its banks, and named the agricultural settlement after himself.

By 1685, several farms had been established, some of them destined to become historic treasures renowned today for their architecture and for their wine.

Stellenbosch, the second-oldest town in South Africa, is also one of delightful contrasts; as a university and cultural centre it's both lively and laid back but − when the traffic and students have left the historic centre − it's easy to travel back in time. A tranquil stroll through oak-lined streets will take you past centuries of well-restored former homes in a variety of classic styles.

STELLENBOSCH,
A NAME SYNONYMOUS WITH WINE
The culture of wine is deeply rooted here. Historical excellence, tradition and continuity combine with up-to-the-minute technology, innovation and international co-operation to form a unique mosaic.

Way back in 1971, when South Africa boasted just 40 estates and about 70 co-ops, three visionary Stellenbosch wine farmers opened the first wine route, with 14 producer members. This vanguard effort was hugely successful, increased sales dramatically,

spawned several other routes, and introduced the concept of wine tourism to the Cape.

For most visitors, the showcase heritage estates and specialist red-wine cellars are what draw them to Stellenbosch, but this town is also the powerhouse of the industry. Giant wholesaler **Distell**, along with the big wine companies and the go-ahead negociants, provide a multinational buzz that is not found in other regions.

Stellenbosch wines dominate most competitions in South Africa and also garner more overseas awards than those from any other district, although they represent only about 11 per cent of the country's total wine-producing areas.

Waterford, a modern and Mediterranean winery and stylish home of superior red wines.

Stellenbosch, often quoted as the leading red-wine producer, also offers a host of whites, bubblies and fortified wines that qualify for the premier league.

Of the wineries widely regarded as being the best in South Africa, four are found in the Stellenbosch area. These are Kanonkop, Rustenberg, Jordan and Thelema.

MAKING SENSE OF STELLENBOSCH
WHERE TO GO, WHAT TO TASTE

With more than 100 producers in this crowded district, it's easy to be overwhelmed when compiling itineraries for sipping and sightseeing. There are five official Stellenbosch wine routes, which carve up the district into manageable sections, but there are also one or two exceptional wineries that choose not to be members of these routes. Our approach here has been to use the eight major roads to Stellenbosch as guidelines. Some of the significant wine farms and cellars along or off these roads are listed, followed by some situated in two valley wards on the outskirts of the town. Each selection presents an eclectic mix, venues renowned for particular wines, those that welcome groups, boutique wineries, historic farms and a few in breathtaking settings.

All of them make good wines; many make outstanding wines and, most importantly, they all welcome visitors without prior appointment.

HEADING FOR STELLENBOSCH
From the South, via the R310

The R310 leaves the N2, the national coastal road, shortly before Macassar. Among the few wine farms along this stretch are a couple whose fame has spread far beyond the borders of South Africa.

Spier may be tourist orientated, but it is also historic, beautiful and an important winelands stop. Along with good modern wines, there are four restaurants, a farm-stall, luxury hotel and outdoor theatre. Both the cheetah and raptor conservation projects are worth visiting.

Vlottenburg offers a good contrast, being a down-to-earth co-op that produces a wide range of sound and popular wines that are keenly priced.

HEADING FOR STELLENBOSCH
via the Polkadraai Road

This is an old main road from Cape Town to Stellenbosch, via Kuils River. Its official title is the M12 – until it enters the environs of Stellenbosch, where it becomes the R306.

If you get on to the M12 from the R102, you will pass the Langverwacht Road that leaves Kuils River's commercial centre to wind into low hills where the beautifully proportioned **Zevenwacht** manor house perches on a slight rise. Picnics and barbecues, in addition to the wine and cheese, make this a congenial estate for family outings.

Saxenburg is the first estate on the M12, producing premier league red wines, including scintillating Shiraz and a host of interesting blends.

The little estate of **Jacobsdal** has built its international reputation on Pinotage, while the winemaker at **Kanu** is making waves with exciting, award-winning wines.

On the Stellenboschkloof Road, off the R306, is **Overgaauw**, producer of stellar reds and the only Sylvaner in South Africa.

Deep in the kloof is **Jordan**, one of the Cape's top performers whose 1998 Cabernet/Merlot blend was awarded a five-star rating by *Wine* magazine.

Near the junction of the R306 and R310 a flutter of flags embellish the entrance to **Neethlingshof**, a beautiful 17th-century estate that produces wines of a high standard.

Asara, formerly the venerable estate of Verdun, offers visitors fine views along with good wines and a white Port.

HEADING FOR STELLENBOSCH
via the Bottelary Road

The Bottelary Road is a continuation of the R102 – an old trunk road, renamed the M23 after it reaches Kuils River – which wanders eastwards with the Bottelary hills undulating along its southern side.

At the whitewashed **Hazendal** complex, the farm-stead's fine 'holbol' gable pre-empts the treasures within. This is also a child-friendly venue. Neither the wines nor the cuisine will disappoint.

Tucked into the hills is the **Kaapzicht** estate where the Steytler family provides a picnic venue along with excellent Pinotage and other award-winning reds. More good reds wait to be sampled at **Hartenberg** estate, along with appetizing rustic fare.

Across the R304 you will find **Simonsig**, one of Stellenbosch's most successful estates. The Malan family was the first to make a Cap Classique; they helped to start the first wine route, and make consistently good red and white wines, which can be found across the globe.

1. Asara
2. Bergkelder
3. Beyerskloof
4. Clos Malverne
5. De Trafford
6. Delaire
7. Delheim
8. Distell
9. Hartenberg
10. Hazendal
11. Jacobsdal
12. JC Le Roux
13. Joostenberg
14. Jordan
15. Kaapzicht
16. Kanonkop
17. Kanu
18. Klein Zalze
19. L'Avenir
20. Laibach
21. Lanzerac
22. Le Bonheur
23. Lievland
24. Louisvale
25. Middelvlei
26. Morgenhof
27. Muratie
28. Neethlingshof
29. Neil Ellis
30. Overgaauw
31. Rustenberg
32. Saxenburg
33. Simonsig
34. Spier
35. Sylvanvale
36. Thelema
37. Uitkyk
38. Villiera
39. Vlottenburg
40. Vriesenhof
41. Warwick
42. Waterford
43. Zevenwacht

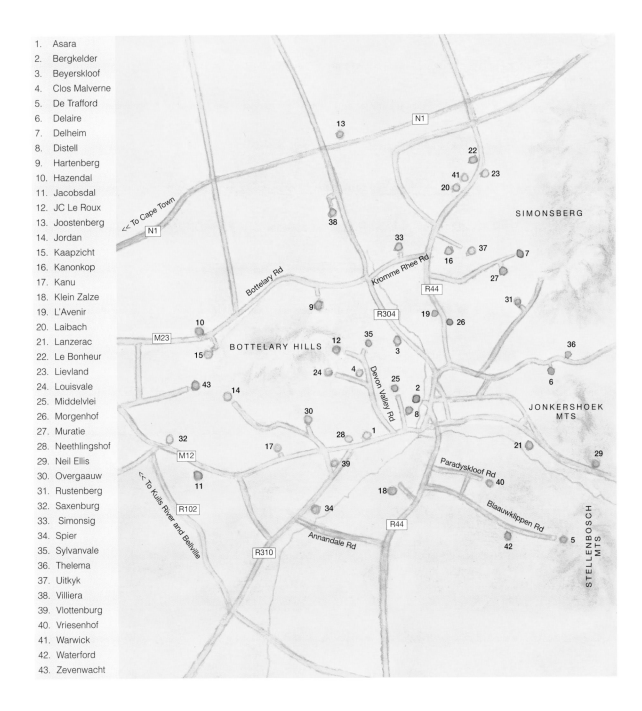

STELLENBOSCH

North of the Bottelary Road, just off the N1, is **Joostenberg**, a child-friendly farm that also boasts one of the oldest surviving Cape farmsteads, which still has its original gable intact. After tasting the wines, picnic in the lavender-lined cellar garden.

HEADING FOR STELLENBOSCH
via the R304

Better known as the Koelenhof Road, this major route to the town passes several wine farms en route from the N1.

One of the most hospitable destinations is **Villiera**, which produces an extensive range of wines that are as affordable as they are popular. This estate is widely regarded as offering the best value for money with both medium- and lower-priced labels.

Nearer to Stellenbosch lies **Beyerskloof**, home to exciting reds, including a Pinotage made by Beyers Truter, one of the Cape's greatest promoters of this indigenous cultivar.

HEADING FOR STELLENBOSCH
from the north, via the R44

The R44 dips under the N1 at Klapmuts, and on its way to Stellenbosch, passes several famous wine farms renowned for reds of superior quality. It is also a route of bewitching beauty.

Lovers of red wine can proceed from **Le Bonheur** to **Lievland**, then cross the road to **Warwick**, which makes a great Chardonnay along with its brilliant red blends. More fine reds await at **Laibach**, a prelude to the stupendous products of the legendary **Kanonkop** estate, where Pinotage reigns supreme.

Uitkyk's small range of wines matches the elegance of its Cape Georgian manor house. And do not miss **Muratie**, off the R44; a 17th-century estate where the sense of history is almost tangible. Pause here to absorb the spirit of the past – and sip the Port after you have sampled the reds.

Delheim, which lies just ahead, provides a contemporary contrast, where groups are received with professional hospitality. Don't miss the Noble Late Harvest when tasting.

A duo of excellent reds and another of whites awaits at the unpretentious **L'Avenir** estate, while **Morgenhof** presents sophisticated charm, its Gallic character reflected in a range of praiseworthy wines and chic coffee-shop fare.

HEADING FOR STELLENBOSCH
From the north, via Helshoogte and the R310

At the summit of the Helshoogte Pass lies **Thelema Mountain Vineyards**, an inspiring place in every respect. The majestic mountains provide an appropriate setting for superb wines that delight palates across the globe.

A little way down the pass is **Delaire** winery, which should be visited for its views alone, where valleys of vines and orchards are backed by soaring mountain crags. The wines complement the restaurant's country fare well.

Rustenberg, one of the most celebrated of Cape estates, sprawls across the Krom River valley on the slopes of the Simonsberg. The estate boasts two historic houses, both beautifully proportioned and meticulously restored homesteads. Elegant flagship wines are in keeping with the magnificence of the surroundings, while the fruity Brampton range is more accessible.

The tasting room at Muratie, where a patina of the past cloaks walls and woodwork with an intriguing aura.

THE JONKERSHOEK VALLEY

This valley, home of the Eerste River, houses a number of secluded wineries, such as that of **Neil Ellis**, whose stylish wines attract star ratings.

Historic **Lanzerac** is as well known for its luxurious hotel as for its wines.,

DEVON VALLEY

The compact ward of Devon Valley, established in 1997, is reached via the Adam Tas Road off the R306, at the outskirts to Stellenbosch.

This enchanting valley presents wines across the spectrum, and is home to two restaurants, adding up to a mini-route of its own.

Start at the top of the hill with a tasting of bubblies at **JC Le Roux**, the country's only 'house of sparkling wine'. Follow with **Sylvanvale**'s vine-dried wines at the Devon Valley Hotel, then head south to sip Chardonnay at **Louisvale**, and award-winning reds at **Clos Malverne**.

At **Middelvlei**, a venerable farm that still keeps suburbia at bay, the Momberg family continues the tradition of producing stylish, characterful red wine.

Middelvlei's charming century-old farmstead, home to the Mombergs.

HEADING FOR STELLENBOSCH
from the south, via the R44

Most of the wine farms along this road are dealt with in the following chapter on the Helderberg. Just outside Stellenbosch, however, the Blaauwklippen Road snakes up into the mountains, lined by wineries and herb nurseries. Two important destinations can be found here: **Waterford**, a Mediterranean-style venue that produces wonderful reds, and further up the slope **De Trafford Wines**, one of Stellenbosch's – and South Africa's – top performers.

VALLEY PRODUCE

Although there are still orchards among the vines, the Stellenbosch region is probably better known for berries than other fruit today. Strawberry farms and roadside stalls are interspersed with the wine farms on more than one route to Stellenbosch, while many berry varieties are cultivated at Hillcrest Berry Orchards.

Red wines characterized by berry flavours make natural partners for berries destined to sauce meat and poultry dishes. Chefs spice and reduce the combination to produce mouthwatering results.

Interesting cheeses and olive oil can be found at farmstalls dotted along the roads to town, along with organic greens and vegetables.

FINE FARE IN STELLENBOSCH

Although there is a wealth of gastronomic venues in and around Stellenbosch, offering a wide choice of cuisines, few are gourmet destinations. Fine fare, fast fare: sidewalk cafés and pubs serving substantial affordable food attest to the fact that most establishments are catering to some 15 000 students.

Diners looking for heritage Cape classics should book for the buffet at the **Jonkershuis** at Spier, or the à la carte version at **De Volkskombuis** in Stellenbosch itself.

Up-market contemporary treats are on the menu at **33 Stellenbosch** on the Vlottenburg Road, and good fare with country flair makes the **Devon Valley Hotel** an inviting venue where the views from the terrace tables compete with the menu.

Decameron is the local landmark for Italian specialities. And for Gallic authenticity, head for the **Joostenberg Bistro** on the R304 at Muldersvlei.

Savour al fresco meals on the **Lanzerac** hotel terrace, or tuck into fruity fare at the **Hillcrest Berry Orchards** restaurant, which uses organically grown produce.

Alternatively, book for one of the winery restaurants. The Guinea Fowl at Saxenburg aspires to gourmet standards, while most try to please both palate and purse.

Recommended are the restaurants at **Blaauwklippen**, **The Duck Pond** at Welmoed, **The Green Door** at Delaire, **The Guinea Fowl** at Saxenburg, **The Hermitage** at Hazendal, **Louiesenhof**, **Morgenhof** and **The Taphuis Grill** at Spier.

MUST SEE PLACES

Where else in the world can you experience life in the 17th century, or just before World War 2, simply by walking a few street blocks? That typical examples of houses from these and other periods are found within so small an area is nothing short of miraculous. The Village Museum in Stellenbosch comprises four dwellings and their gardens, illustrating different architectural periods over three and a half centuries. The thatched **Schreuderhuis** (left) is the oldest, an example of a pioneer settler home, while the gabled **Blettermanhuis** reflects the more elegant lifestyle of wealthy residents toward the end of the 18th century. **Grosvenor House** dates from about 1800, and the **Berghuis** is a typical Victorian residence.

Schreuderhuis, oldest house in the Village Museum Complex in Stellenbosch.

STELLENBOSCH

CHICKEN SALAD WITH FRUIT AND NUTS

This delectably simple salad comes from 33 Stellenbosch, on the Vlottenburg Road.

1 butter lettuce, washed and dried
2 red lettuce, washed and dried
100 g tatsoi
100 g red mustard leaves
100 g rocket leaves
50 g celery stalks, chopped
4 sweet oranges, cut into segments and membranes removed
2 Granny Smith apples, cored and cut into thin wedges
500 g grilled chicken breast, diced or sliced
300 g pecan nut halves

DRESSING

1 egg
5 ml (1 tsp) hot English mustard powder
120 ml (8 tbsp) white-wine vinegar
120 ml (8 tbsp) balsamic vinegar
300 ml extra virgin olive oil
100 ml honey
100 ml Dijon mustard
salt and pepper to taste

First make the dressing. Place the egg and mustard powder in the bowl of a blender or food processor and mix. Then add the white-wine vinegar, balsamic vinegar, oil, honey and Dijon mustard and blend or process until smooth. Season with salt and pepper.

Break all the greens into bite-sized pieces and divide them equally between 6 plates. Sprinkle the celery over, then arrange the orange segments and apple wedges on the salad, and top with the chicken. Drizzle over the dressing, and sprinkle with pecan nuts.

Serves 6

VARIATION: Replace grilled chicken with smoked chicken breast.

THE ICA WATERBLOMMETJIE AND ANCHOVY GRATIN WITH SPARKLING WINE VELOUTÉ

As winter draws to an end, waterblommetjies *(Aponogeton distachyus), bloom in Boland dams and rivers. Once used by the Khoisan tribes, these flowers are today cultivated commercially as well, and continue to add a delicate flavour to time-honoured bredies (stews) and soups. Today's chefs are also using them in original and contemporary ways. The Institute of Culinary Arts (ICA) outside Stellenbosch, the largest private chefs' training centre in South Africa, contributes expertise to various winelands restaurants when required. This novel recipe, created for JC le Roux in the Devon Valley, combines* waterblommetjies *and sparkling wine in a Provençal-type gratin with a luxurious sauce.*

GRATIN	VELOUTÉ SAUCE
12 large fresh waterblommetjies, blanched	25 ml (5 tsp) butter
12 anchovy fillets	40 ml (8 tsp) flour
50 g breadcrumbs	250 ml (1 cup) vegetable stock
50 g Parmesan cheese, grated	100 ml dry sparkling wine
finely grated zest of ½ lemon	50 g cold butter, diced
black pepper	60 ml (4 tbsp) thick cream
20 ml (4 tsp) butter, melted	lemon juice to taste

For the gratin, preheat the grill to hot. Place the *waterblommetjies* on a baking tray and top each with an anchovy fillet. Combine the breadcrumbs, cheese and lemon zest and grind black pepper over. Sprinkle the mixture over the *waterblommetjies,* then drizzle with melted butter and grill until the crust is golden brown. For the velouté sauce, heat the butter, add the flour and stir to form a roux. Stir in the vegetable stock, bring to a simmer and simmer for 8–10 minutes to reduce slightly. Add the sparkling wine, then whisk in the diced cold butter. When completely dissolved, stir in the cream. Season the sauce with lemon juice to taste and serve with the gratin.

Serves 6

HILLCREST BERRY ORCHARDS
RASPBERRY MUFFINS

4 x 250 ml (4 cups) cake flour

10 ml (2 tsp) baking powder

250 ml (1 cup) sugar

pinch of salt

40 ml (8 tsp) butter

10 ml (2 tsp) honey

10 ml (2 tsp) treacle

10 ml (2 tsp) bicarbonate of soda

2 eggs

60 ml (4 tbsp) oil

375 ml (1½ cups) milk

fresh or frozen raspberries

Preheat the oven to 180 °C.

Sift together the flour, baking powder, sugar and salt.

In a small saucepan, combine the butter, honey and treacle and bring just to the boil (do not cook).

Add the bicarbonate of soda and allow to fizz.

Beat the eggs, whisk in the oil and add to the milk, stirring to combine. Add the milk mixture to the dry ingredients and mix gently. Do not over mix. Fold in the butter and honey mixture lightly.

Place a dessertspoonful of batter into each muffin mould. Add 3–4 frozen or fresh raspberries.

Fill each mould with batter to three-quarters full and bake for 15–20 minutes.

Makes 18 small or 6 large muffins

NOTE: It is important not to mix in the berries since they 'stain' the mixture.
If using frozen berries, do not thaw them first.

DECADENT CHOCOLATE CAKE

Craig Cormack is one of the Cape's most personable and friendly chefs, whose considerable culinary talents are only revealed when diners tuck into his fare at Figaro, on the Spier estate. Chef Cormack warms the cake before serving it, but serve it at room temperature if you prefer.

125 g butter
500 g plain dark semi-sweet chocolate
(such as Albany)
5 large eggs, separated

7 ml (1½ tsp) cake flour
7 ml (1½ tsp) white sugar
morello cherry sauce or coulis to serve (optional)
homemade vanilla ice cream to serve (optional)

Preheat the oven to 160 °C.
Melt the butter and chocolate together over low heat. Remove from the heat. Add the egg yolks and mix in the flour and the sugar. Whisk the egg whites until stiff peaks form and fold them into the batter.
Line a 25-cm-diameter springform cake pan with baking parchment and oil lightly. Pour in the batter.
Bake the cake for 45 minutes, then turn off the oven and leave the cake in the oven for an extra 10–15 minutes.
Cool in the pan, then transfer carefully to a wire cooling rack and cool completely.
If cherries are in season, make the sauce by simmering 500 g fresh cherries in a medium or heavy sugar suryp, depending on tartness, for 5–10 minutes until tender. Finish with a little brandy if desired. Frozen or canned cherries can also be used – adjust cooking times.
Serve the cake cut into wedges, accompanied by a cherry or other berry coulis and a scoop of vanilla ice cream.
Alternatively, you can serve it on its own with espresso coffee.

Makes 1 x 25 cm cake

HELDERBERG

ABOVE *The Helderberg and Vergelegen.*

OPPOSITE *Vergelegen manor house (1);
Blaauwklippen (2); Vergenoegd Cellar (3); Lady
Phillips restaurant (4); 96 Winery Road restaurant (5).*

Lucky indeed are those who call this
stretch of land home. Slotted in between
the curved white beaches of False Bay
and the magnificent Helderberg
mountain range, with its eight distinctive
peaks, are coastal towns and verdant
rural pockets in a captivating setting.

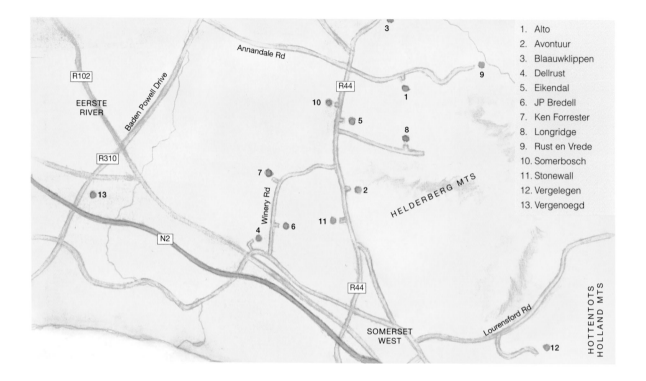

1. Alto
2. Avontuur
3. Blaauwklippen
4. Dellrust
5. Eikendal
6. JP Bredell
7. Ken Forrester
8. Longridge
9. Rust en Vrede
10. Somerbosch
11. Stonewall
12. Vergelegen
13. Vergenoegd

Not only do the residents live in glorious surroundings and enjoy a balmy climate, but they are blessed with farmstalls that stock dew-fresh produce and a harbour where wriggling fish are landed on the quay. Even olive oil is bought at source – produced at Morgenster, one of the loveliest Cape Dutch farms in the Boland.

In fact, deciding which wine should accompany this bounty is one of the harder tasks for Helderberg residents, and it is carried out in the smug knowledge that some of South Africa's finest wine is produced on the fertile slopes around them.

Visitors to the region can share more than a soupçon of this bounty, and the bustling dormitory town of Somerset West makes an excellent base for wine and angling excursions and for visits to historic farms, the nature reserve and the gastronomic meccas of the Helderberg.

The fabric of the rural past lives on in a tiny corner of the town, which formed its centre early in the 19th century. The Dutch Reformed Church and graveyard dream on across the grass of Nagmaal (Communion) Square, opposite the old parsonage, which houses a popular restaurant today.

The Strand and Gordon's Bay are popular seaside resorts, while near the historic Sir Lowry's Pass village the N2 starts its climb up the equally historic pass to the hinterland. Railway buffs can indulge in nostalgic steam trips on this route.

WINING AND DINING IN THE HELDERBERG

French, German, Italian, Austrian and Greek fare can be found on the menus of Helderberg's restaurants, reflecting the cosmopolitan nature of its population. Given the proximity of the ocean, it is not surprising that other establishments specialize in fish and seafood. Gastronomes can indulge in haute cuisine or contemporary fare, and savour al fresco lunches such as those served at **Blaauwklippen** and **Eikendal** vineyards. **Avontuur** estate also presents well-priced country buffets as well as panoramic views from the terrace.

One of the greatest success stories – and deservedly so – is the restaurant at **96 Winery Road**, which is also its name. This rustic venue on a farm off the R44 presents flavourful fare that is trendy but never over the top. The wine list focuses on local stars before listing others, and there is a walk-in cellar for connoisseurs.

Close by is **l'Auberge du Paysan**, an authentic Gallic destination in the Boland, that offers classic haute cuisine with a nod to the bounty of the Cape.

In the historic heart of Somerset West, **Die Ou Pastorie** – a former parsonage – houses a restaurant noted for its innovative, up-to-the-minute menu, ably matched by an informative wine list.

At the breathtaking Vergelegen, an essential destination on every itinerary, the **Lady Phillips** serves stylish lunches and teas seven days a week. During the summer months, **The Rose Garden**'s light fare offers solace to those who forgot to reserve a table at the very popular Lady Phillips.

WINES OF THE HELDERBERG

Vineyards cover many of the long slopes that lead from the foothills of the Helderberg mountains to the coastal plain. The vines, cooled by sea breezes, enjoy a practically perfect climate for the production of fine wines, a marketing truism that has been borne out many times by the 20-odd producers.

Their farms stretch from the Schapenberg slopes in the foothills of the Hottentots Holland Mountains in the north, to the vineyards close to the beaches of False Bay in the south. Local and international investment in vines is under way, which will see the number of labels increase in the future.

Visitors have a good choice of both white and red wines to sample in cellars that range from large historic establishments to boutique New World cellars. Few of the latter, unfortunately, are open to the public without prior appointment, so they are not included here.

Vergelegen is widely regarded as being one of the top five producers of white and red wine in the country, and **Rust en Vrede** is one of the top five producers of red wine.

Some producers of fine white wines: Avontuur, Eikendal (Chardonnay), Ken Forrester (Chenin Blanc; tastings at his restaurant, 96 Winery Road), Longridge (open summer months only), Vergelegen.

Some producers of fine red wines: Alto, Avontuur, Blaauwklippen, JP Bredell, Dellrust, Eikendal, Helderkruin, Longridge (open summer months only), Rust en Vrede estate, Somerbosch, Stonewall, Vergelegen, Vergenoegd.

Producers of good Port: Alto, JP Bredell, Dellrust, Vergenoegd.

Historic venues include Vergelegen and Vergenoegd.

Hospitable venues that cater for crowds include: Avontuur, Blaauwklippen (a transport museum is an additional attraction), Eikendal and Vergelegen.

VEGETABLE PANINI

The restaurant on Avontuur estate offers appetizing breakfast fare, along with buffet and à la carte lunches. This colourful and delicious open sandwich doubles as starter or light main course, and is favoured by vegetarians. Bottled peppadews can be found at delis, farmstalls and in supermarkets.

1 red sweet pepper, seeded and roughly chopped
1 orange sweet pepper, seeded and roughly chopped
1 baby marrow (courgette), trimmed and sliced diagonally
1 small or ½ medium brinjal (aubergine or eggplant), thickly sliced diagonally

olive oil
salt and black pepper
1 panini or small ciabatta bread, halved horizontally
50 g homemade feta cheese, drained and crumbled
30 ml (2 tbsp) basil pesto
4 peppadews, drained

Preheat the oven to 220 °C.

Arrange the peppers, the baby marrow and brinjal slices in a single layer in a shallow baking pan. Drizzle evenly with oil and season with salt and pepper.

Roast the vegetables until just limp, then remove and cool to room temperature.

Crisp the panini or ciabatta halves in the oven.

Divide the vegetables between the bread halves and top with the feta cheese. Spoon the basil pesto evenly over both, and top with 2 peppadews each.

Serve with a side helping of crisp garden salad, tossed with a tangy dressing of your choice.

Serves 1–2

CHICKEN WITH TOMATO JAM

96 Winery Road is a warm, welcoming country restaurant with an impressive walk-in wine cellar.
It is a favourite venue among both locals and visitors to the area. This flavourful chicken dish, typical of
Chef Natasha Harris's appetizing and uncomplicated fare, is one you will enjoy trying in your own kitchen.

4 boned chicken breasts
8 fresh sage leaves
4−8 slices mozzarella cheese
4−8 slices prosciutto, pancetta or good smoked ham
butter

TOMATO JAM
olive oil
2 onions, peeled and coarsely chopped
4 ripe tomatoes, roughly chopped
250 ml (1 cup) sugar
125 ml (½ cup) white-wine vinegar

First make the jam. Heat a little olive oil in a heavy-based saucepan. Add the onion and cook, stirring occasionally, until tender but not browned. Add the tomatoes and continue cooking over low heat for 5 minutes. Add the sugar and the vinegar and simmer for about 40 minutes, or until the jam starts to darken and 5 ml (1 tsp) of the mixture placed in cold water becomes sticky. Cool the jam to room temperature. Preheat the oven to 180 °C.
Cut through the chicken breasts horizontally. Spread one half of each liberally with tomato jam, sandwich with the other half and spread with more jam. Top each breast with 2 sage leaves, then cover with 1−2 slices of cheese (depending on the size of the cheese slices). Cover the cheese completely with 1−2 slices of ham. Transfer the chicken to a baking dish. Top each chicken breast with a blob of butter and bake for 30−40 minutes, or until cooked through.

Serves 4

LADY PHILLIPS STARTER
OF SMOKED SALMON ON BLINIS

This restaurant, on the historic Vergelegen estate, is one of the
most popular restaurants in the Cape for summer luncheons.
Former executive chef Joanne van Staden liked to add an oriental note to her dishes,
which were also characterized by the use of locally produced fresh and seasonal ingredients.

500 g smoked Franschhoek salmon trout
60 g herbed or plain cream cheese
30 ml (2 tbsp) pressed caviar
6 sprigs fresh dill
60 g mizuna, mibuna and flowering kale or mixed
baby salad leaves
60 g pecan nuts, toasted
150 ml oriental-style dressing (see below)
6 blinis (see alongside)

BLINIS
125 g mashed potato
salt and white pepper
25 ml (5 tsp) cream
25 ml (5 tsp) butter
2 egg whites
1 sprig fresh dill, chopped
5 ml (1 tsp) garlic and ginger purée

Preheat the oven to 160 °C.
First make the blinis. Season the mashed potatoes well, add the cream and butter. Whisk the egg whites
until they form soft peaks and fold them into the mashed potato mixture together with the dill and the
garlic and ginger purée.
Spoon the batter into 6 oiled muffin pans and bake for 10−12 minutes.
For the oriental-style dressing, combine 30 ml (2 tbsp) fresh lemon or lime juice with 30 ml (2 tbsp) light soy sauce,
preferably Kikkoman. Whisk in 90 ml (6 tbsp) sunflower oil until the mixture emulsifies.
To assemble, fold 6 slices of smoked salmon trout in half horizonally and roll up.
Place a roll on top of each warm blini. Top with cream cheese and garnish with caviar and a sprig of dill.
Surround each blini with mizuna, mibuna and flowering kale or baby salad leaves and toasted pecan nuts
and a drizzle of oriental dressing.

Serves 6

ELDERBERG

PAARL AND WELLINGTON

Paarl, the pearl of the Boland, boasts many attractions, but for the gastronomic traveller, it's the delicious diversity of products from this broad and beautiful valley that is particularly tempting.

ABOVE *Nederburg by night.*

OPPOSITE *La Concorde (1); KWV's Cathedral Cellar (2); Bosman's (3); Agter-Paarl wine estates (4); Pontac (5); Laborie (6); goat tower on the Fairview estate (7).*

A cursory look at the range of wines produced reveals excellent reds, award-winning whites and fortified stars – along with the only kosher wine and one of the few organic wines produced in South Africa.

Turn to the cuisine and you are equally as spoilt for choice: gourmet menus await epicures, while venues offering portable feasts, hearty *boerekos* and contemporary Cape fare make decisions a delightful dilemma.

This cornucopia of culinary treasures lies in the Drakenstein valley, some 56 kilometres from Cape Town along the N1. Take the turnoff to the town and you will slow down, literally and figuratively, as you wend your way down the 11-kilometre long Main Street.

The Cape architectural styles of three centuries are reflected in the buildings lining the road, interspersed here and there with a town vineyard that stretches from the pavement up the steep slopes of Paarl mountain.

The mountain itself is an integral facet of the scene, topped by gigantic granite boulders that have stood sentinel over the valley for 500 million years. Known as Skilpad (tortoise) Mountain by the original nomadic inhabitants, 17th-century Dutch Company officials renamed the boulders Diamond and Pearl when they saw them glistening in the morning dew.

The Berg River is the lifeblood of Paarl and the Drakenstein valley, an irrigation artery that has inspired affection beyond its agricultural importance. Venerable farms near its banks are revered as the source of the Afrikaans language movement, and patriots identify the river's flow with that of Afrikaner history.

The historic and hospitable Rhebokskloof estate offers a wide range of wines and good food in a setting of vineyards, orchards and fynbos.

PAARL AND WELLINGTON

Perched on the slopes of Paarl Mountain, the Grande Roche hotel offers unabashed luxury, superb service and gourmet fare.

PAARL PRODUCE AND CUISINE

Full advantage is taken of the Mediterranean climate – hot, dry summers and cool, wet winters – by farmers who produce deciduous fruit, table grapes and olives, for oil and for the table. The region is also home to some excellent cheeses, including a fine selection of goat's-milk varieties, as well as successful strawberry growers and a fresh-water crayfish farm.

Diners will find it easy to team their choice of cuisine with one of Paarl's fine wines – local produce and regional labels make excellent partners.

When the occasion calls for a gastronomic treat, diners have a choice of up-market venues to consider, while several wineries operate informal eateries that serve seasonal fare at pleasing prices, and others offer picnics during the summer months.

Grande Roche, recognized globally as one of Africa's outstanding hotels, has garnered a long list of local and international awards. **Bosman's** restaurant, housed in the gracious manor house, can boast its own collection of trophies for cuisine and wine list, service and appointments.

Before they make their selection, diners need to decide which menu to peruse. Executive chef Frank Zlomke presents seafood, gourmet, Cape-flavoured, vegetarian, low-fat and à la carte menus every day, and they all change daily. Whatever you opt for, you are assured of classically plated food that is fresh and flavourful, served with professional formality.

Just a stone's throw away is **Pontac Manor**, a country hotel with an intriguing past, whose beautiful Victorian farmstead oozes timeless hospitality. The restaurant, housed in former outbuildings, serves fine fare in contemporary Cape mode. The satiny sauces that chef Abe Conradie favours are worth every scrumptious kilojoule …

Among the farms that hug the western slopes of the Paarl mountain, Seidelberg estate perpetuates the farm's

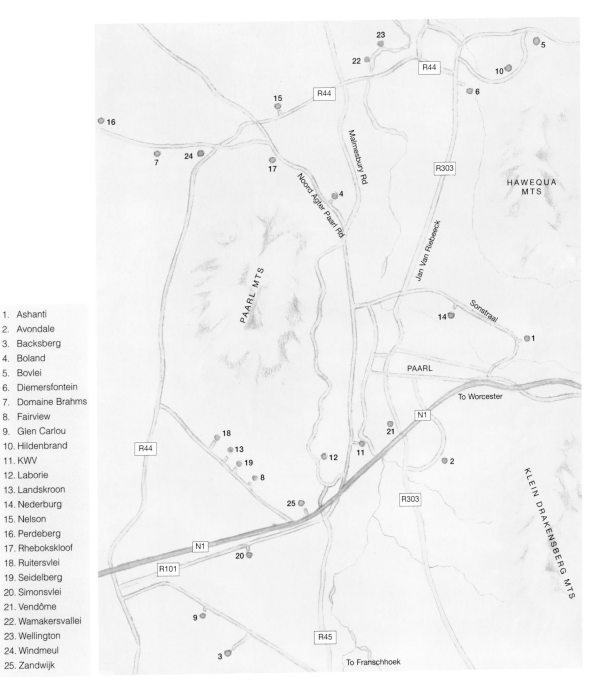

1. Ashanti
2. Avondale
3. Backsberg
4. Boland
5. Bovlei
6. Diemersfontein
7. Domaine Brahms
8. Fairview
9. Glen Carlou
10. Hildenbrand
11. KWV
12. Laborie
13. Landskroon
14. Nederburg
15. Nelson
16. Perdeberg
17. Rhebokskloof
18. Ruitersvlei
19. Seidelberg
20. Simonsvlei
21. Vendôme
22. Wamakersvallei
23. Wellington
24. Windmeul
25. Zandwijk

original name with both the resaurant and a range of wine called **De Leuwen Jagt** (the lion hunt).

As chef Michael Mandy has to compete with breathtaking views from the terrace and the attraction of glass-blowing by two talented artists inside, his menu of contemporary country fare is as appetising as it is prettily plated.

Among the farms of Agter-Paarl, none is more beautiful than **Rhebokskloof**, which has vines stretching to the border of the mountain nature reserve. This estate, with its two welcoming restaurants and the winery, has been operating for more than three centuries.

THE WINES OF PAARL
WHERE TO GO, WHAT TO TASTE
There are about 40 producers in the district. Of these, two are probably better known than the rest: **KWV International**, which is not only the largest co-operative winery in the world but also an organization that controlled the Cape wine industry for the best part of a century. Today it focuses more on exports, but visitors are well catered for with cellar tours and tastings, a coffee shop and a wine emporium that stocks the various ranges, from the up-market Cathedral Cellar to the easy-drinking, affordable Robert's Rock labels. Fortified wines and Cape brandies are also on sale.

To the north of Paarl lies the **Nederburg** estate, which is just as well known for its wine auction as it is for its consistently good wines and exceptional Late Harvest dessert wines.

In addition to the Paarl Wine Route, travellers can focus on the Red Route, which was launched by Paarl Vintners, the region's marketing association, to highlight the many fine reds produced. The area has long attracted adventurous winemakers, and this is certainly true today, with new players – most of them small – entering the scene even as pioneer farms surge ahead to meet the challenges of the new millennium.

Fairview is widely regarded as being one of the four most exciting wineries in South Africa, and **Boland Kelder** is seen as one of a handful of cellars offering the best value for budget-priced wines.

De Oude Paarl Wijnhuis is a good venue for visitors with no time to tour, as the wines of the members of Paarl Vintners are available for tasting and are sold at farm prices. The centre houses an up-market and casual terrace restaurant widening the choice of main street dining venues.

Keeping to wineries that welcome visitors without prior appointments, here are a few suggestions for DIY itineraries:

Producers of good sparkling wine: Backsberg, Laborie, Nederburg.

Some producers of good whites: Fairview, Laborie, Nederburg, Rhebokskloof, Seidelberg, Simonsvlei.

Some producers of good reds: Ashanti, Avondale, Boland Kelder, Domaine Brahms, Fairview, Glen Carlou, Perdeberg Co-op, Ruitersvlei, Seidelberg, Simonsvlei, Windmeul Co-op.

Producers of good port: Glen Carlou, KWV International, Landskroon.

Historic venues include: Laborie, Nederburg, Zandwijk (produces Kleine Draken kosher wines).

Intimate boutique wineries: Glen Carlou; Vendôme.

Hospitable venues that cater for crowds: Ashanti, Backsberg, Boland Kelder, Fairview, KWV International, Nelson, Simonsvlei, Seidelberg.

Child-friendly wineries: Backsberg, Boland Kelder, Fairview, Landskroon, Rhebokskloof.

WELLINGTON

A FASCINATING MIX OF CONSERVATIVE TRADITION AND ENERGETIC ENTERPRISE

After visiting Paarl, many travellers head for the hinterland over Du Toitskloof Pass or turn south towards Franschhoek, thus missing out on a delightful, largely undiscovered part of the Berg River valley – not to mention diverse and exciting wines.

Originally known as Limiet Vallei (the boundary or limit of settler civilization), and later renamed Wagenmakersvallei (wagon makers' valley), several of the Huguenot farms founded here at the tail-end of the 17th century are still owned and worked by the descendants of those refugees. A few farms have remained quite unspoilt, hidden treasures dreaming on in beguiling settings, that the curious visitor can find with a little effort.

The central point is the village of Wellington – rural and conservative, but hospitable – that lies at the foot of the Groenberg. In 1863 it enjoyed a burst of publicity as the first destination of the railway line carrying steam trains out of Cape Town.

VALLEY PRODUCE AND AL FRESCO FEASTS

It's worth finding a lofty viewpoint to take in the orchards, vines, fields and pastures that yield the mixed produce of this fertile valley.

Deciduous fruits and table grapes are grown for the fresh market, but a lot of produce is also dried; Wellington is the headquarters of the Cape dried-fruit industry.

The valley is also home to several vine nurseries, or *stokkies* (vine cuttings) farms, as they are known.

Wellington sprawls across the foot of the Groenberg.

Vast stretches of silvery olive orchards that shimmer in the heat supply a major part of the table olives found on local supermarket shelves. Alongside you can see fields of buchu bushes, an indigenous Cape herb that is enjoying renewed popularity both locally and overseas. Buchu's medicinal qualities were known to the early nomadic inhabitants of the area, who shared their knowledge with the European settlers. Today brandy, vinegar and tonic water made from buchu are all in demand, and the oil fetches very high prices.

Indigenous and traditional Cape specialities can be found on the menu of a unique outdoor 'restaurant' in the foothills of the Hawequa Mountains, east of Wellington. Here, between huge granite boulders, is a shady clearing where **Kontreikos in the Fynbos** operates in good weather, serving country fare to guests who arrive on horseback, by tractor and trailer, or by car, after tasting wines on surrounding farms.

The restaurant at **Diemersfontein** offers a contrast, presenting up-market food that is quality controlled by talented Franschhoek chef Matthew Gordon.

THE WINES OF WELLINGTON

These can be grouped into two broad categories. Firstly, there are the cheerful, value-for-money labels produced mainly by the co-operatives, many of which complement the robust and rustic regional fare to perfection.

The co-ops, most of which open on Saturdays, make up the majority of stops on the wine route, offering both delicious whites and easy-drinking reds, designed to boost export sales. These are great places to stock up with affordable wines for everyday quaffing.

If time is short, head for **Bovlei** (try the juicy Cabernet), **Wamakersvallei Winery** and **Wellington Co-op**, and be aware that many of the enjoyable fruity reds are also high-alcohol wines.

The second group consists of about 10 producers of up-market labels, some of them overseas investors, who have already succeeded in putting Wellington on the international wine map as a red region to watch. Many of them are not open to the public, so they are not included here, but this could change.

If powerful reds please your palate, head for **Diemersfontein** farm, which also boasts beautiful gardens and an elegant country guesthouse. A visit here is a multifaceted experience: along with a team dedicated to making the best in site-specific reds, there are also walking and horse-riding, art and local music to savour.

Just as welcoming is **Hildenbrand Estate**, named after its vivacious owner – winemaker and viticulturist Reni Hildenbrand. Her wines are as exciting and individual as their creator, and there are also olives and olive oil to taste and Mediterranean lunches to relish.

Diemersfontein offers visitors a guesthouse, wine tasting and country fare in a beautiful garden setting.

MARINATED GOAT'S-MILK CHEESE

Here is a simple but delicious combination of produce from the Paarl region,
perfect as a starter for a buffet table. Serve with crusty bread.

450 g firm goat's-milk cheese, cut into blocks   fresh thyme sprigs
pitted black olives   1–2 fresh red chillies, halved lengthways
fresh rosemary sprigs   300 ml extra-virgin olive oil

Layer the cheese and olives in a glass jar, tuck in the herbs and chillies and then pour over the olive oil to cover.
Screw on the lid, then leave the mixture for a day or two – or for up to a fortnight in the fridge – before using.

RHEBOKSKLOOF SMOKED OSTRICH FILLET WITH GOAT'S-MILK CHEESE AND OLIVE MOUSSE

We have simplifed this gourmet recipe slightly for home use. It is the creation of Andreas Roscher, a former executive chef of Rhebokskloof in Agter-Paarl, an estate that makes excellent use of local ingredients.

500 g ostrich fillet, lightly smoked if desired
50 ml extra-virgin olive oil
a sprig of thyme
a sprig of rosemary

MOUSSE
1 medium onion, peeled and finely chopped
120 g chevin (French-style goat's-milk cheese)
50 g pitted Calamata olives
a bunch of chives, snipped

RICE CAKES
200 g cooked basmati rice
1 egg, separated
15 ml (1 tbsp) chopped fresh coriander leaves
15 ml (1 tbsp) cornflour
salt and pepper

JUNIPER BERRY SAUCE
1 onion, peeled and finely chopped
150 ml fresh cream
15 ml (1 tbsp) crushed juniper berries
150 ml beef stock
50 g cold butter, diced

Preheat the oven to 180 °C.

Cut the ostrich into 4 x 125 g medallions. Heat a little of the olive oil in a pan until very hot, then seal the fillets on both sides. Remove and set aside.

Make the rice cakes by combining the rice with the egg yolk, coriander and cornflour. Whisk the egg white and fold it in. Season with salt and pepper. Shape into 4 flattish cakes and bake in the preheated oven until golden brown.

For the mousse, add the chopped onion to the pan, and sauté until tender. Leave to cool, then mix with the remaining ingredients. Transfer the ostrich medallions to a roasting pan, pat mousse onto top of meat, tuck in the thyme and rosemary and roast for about 6 minutes, or until medium rare.

For the sauce, heat a little more olive oil, add the onion and sauté until soft. Add the cream and crushed juniper berries and reduce the mixture by one third. Stir in the stock and simmer for 2 minutes. Strain the sauce, then blend until smooth. Stir the diced butter into the sauce, one piece at a time. Keep warm.

When ready to serve, place a rice cake in the centre of each of 4 plates, top each with a medallion of ostrich, then surround with the juniper berry sauce and seasonal vegetables of your choice.

Serves 4

P AARL AND WELLINGTON

WELLINGTON LAMB KNUCKLE WITH DRIED FRUIT

Katrina Steytler is an expert horsewoman, a qualified tour guide, can switch happily from English to French or Afrikaans, and is an experienced hiker and a good cook. This recipe is an adaptation of one of her signature dishes, which she makes in a large black cast-iron pot. The sweet-sour flavours are a heritage of 18th-century Dutch colonial tastes. Fruit was often added to meat dishes by Cape Malay cooks, who also introduced the settlers to the liberal use of spices. This is one of those dishes that taste better if made a day ahead.

500 g mixed dried fruit, prunes pitted
vegetable oil
6 onions, peeled, sliced and the slices halved
2 red sweet peppers, seeded, cored and sliced
2 yellow sweet peppers, seeded, cored and sliced
15–30 ml (1–2 tbsp) brown sugar
5 ml (1 tsp) each turmeric, grated nutmeg and
medium-strength curry powder
2 kg lamb knuckles

30 ml (2 tbsp) seasoned flour
4–6 cloves garlic, crushed with a little salt
8 whole cloves
6 sticks cinnamon
10 ml (2 tsp) grated fresh ginger or ground ginger
375 ml (1½ cups) lamb or beef stock, warmed
salt and freshly ground black pepper
15 ml (1 tbsp) smooth apricot jam
red-wine vinegar or lemon juice

Pour over enough water to just cover the dried fruit and set aside. Preheat the oven to 190 °C. Heat a little oil in a large, heavy-based saucepan or Dutch oven, add the onions and sauté until starting to wilt. Stir in the peppers and sauté, stirring occasionally, until the vegetables are tender and the onions golden. While the vegetables are cooking, combine the sugar, turmeric, nutmeg and curry powder and mix well. In a small pan, heat 10 ml (2 tsp) oil, add the spice mixture, and stir briskly until aromatic. Remove from the stove and set aside.

Remove the onion and pepper mixture from the saucepan, using a slotted spoon. Shake the lamb knuckles with the seasoned flour in a plastic bag to coat the meat, then add the meat to the remaining oil in the large saucepan, and brown on all sides. You may have to add a little more oil. Return the onion and pepper mixture to the saucepan, then stir in the spiced sugar. Add the garlic, cloves, cinnamon and ginger and stir. Stir in the heated stock, bring the contents of the pan to a simmer then transfer the pan to a preheated oven and bake for 1–1½ hours, or until the meat is tender. Season to taste with salt and ground pepper, then leave to cool. Skim off any fat, then drain the dried fruit and add to the meat mixture. Bring back to a simmer and cook gently on top of the stove or in the oven until the meat is very tender. Stir in the apricot jam, and add vinegar or lemon juice to taste; the flavours should be sweet-sour. Check the seasoning. Serve with rice.

Serves 8

PAARL AND WELLINGTON

PONTAC RESTAURANT FLAMBÉED LAMB KIDNEYS

Executive chef Abe Conradie combines his admiration for classic haute cuisine with a deep love of South African ingredients and heritage dishes. The results are irresistible. He has reintroduced local diners to the joys of offal, as illustrated by this recipe, where the meat is enhanced with good Paarl wine and Port.

800 g lamb kidneys, cleaned

100 ml brandy

25 ml (5 tsp) butter

3 large onions, peeled and thinly sliced

30 ml (2 tbsp) brown sugar

100 ml balsamic vinegar

salt and pepper

15 ml (1 tbsp) Madagascar green peppercorns

150 ml dry red wine

250 ml (1 cup) port

500 ml (2 cups) strong lamb stock

1 sprig fresh rosemary

50 ml (10 tsp) unsalted butter

sunflower oil

Halve each kidney lengthways and cut out the white core. Rinse under cold water, pat dry, then transfer to a bowl and pour half of the brandy over. Set aside to marinate.

Heat the butter in a heavy-based saucepan. Add the onions and cook them slowly, stirring occasionally, until they are tender and starting to caramelize. Add the sugar and balsamic vinegar and continue cooking until the mixture darkens and becomes sticky. Season to taste with salt and pepper.

Place the green peppercorns in a plastic bag and crush them with a rolling pin. Transfer to a small saucepan, add the wine and Port and cook, uncovered, until the mixture is reduced and syrupy. Add the lamb stock and rosemary and reduce by a further third. Whisk in the butter and season to taste. The sauce should be fairly thick and glossy.

Place a little oil in a large frying pan and heat until the oil starts smoking. Drain the kidneys well and discard the marinade. Add the kidneys to the frying pan and sear for at least 1 minute on one side. Do *not* turn the kidneys over or shake the pan, as this will stop the searing process and cause the moisture to 'leak' from the kidneys. Turn the kidneys over, using a pair of tongs, and repeat the process, adding a little extra oil if necessary, until kidneys are cooked to the desired degree. Add the remaining brandy, carefully ignite it and flambé the mixture, shaking the pan until the flame dies down.

Serve the kidneys drizzled with the onion and peppercorn sauce. Serve with vegetables of your choice, or with potato rosti, butternut crisps and fresh rosemary, as Chef Conradie does.

Serves 4 generously

PAARL AND WELLINGTON

FRANSCHHOEK

In this historic and most Gallic corner of the Cape, visitors are guaranteed a bountiful combination of breathtaking scenery, world-class cuisine, fine wines and professional service.

ABOVE *The gracious Boschendal manor.*

OPPOSITE *Boschendal (1); Le Quartier Français (2); La Petite Ferme (3); Rickety Bridge (4); talented chef Margot Janse (5); cellar at La Motte (6).*

It's an irresistible combination that can be savoured while staying in a valley B&B or renowned auberge, a self-catering vineyard cottage or a five-star hotel.

And, should the pleasures of the palate ever pall, your hosts will point you in the direction of charming antique shops and art galleries, or suggest a day of trout fishing in the mountains.

Even the most blasé of travellers take home special memories of excursions such as wine tasting on horse-back: Imagine ambling along mountain trails as the valley mists lift, pausing at boutique cellars to take in heartstopping views while sipping exceptional vintages, and finishing with a portable feast in the vineyards ...

Whether you start out from Cape Town, from Paarl or from Stellenbosch, you will arrive at the R45, which snakes through lush orchards and vineyards to this gastronomic mecca.

The Franschhoek valley is possibly the Cape's most spectacular wine region. The valley farms and picturesque town of Franschhoek are sheltered by the towering peaks of the Wemmershoek, Groot Drakenstein and Franschhoek mountain ranges, adding up to a series of majestic backdrops at every compass point.

En route to the town, whitewashed façades of Cape Dutch farmsteads shine through the trees, their grand entrances adorned with Gallic names that celebrate the French Huguenot ancestry of their founders.

These 17th-century refugees introduced quality viti-culture to the Cape, and also left a wider legacy of huge clans of descendants bearing names that are common all over South Africa today.

A good winter rainfall and the bountiful Berg River ensure that this is indeed a valley of plenty, as well known for its deciduous fruit as for its viticulture.

Summer visitors are spoilt for choice as farmstalls tempt with trays of perfect plums, golden peaches and rosy nectarines, while autumn sees valley orchards yield apples and pears of excellent quality.

Franschhoek's most popular delicacy is the salmon trout reared at the **Three Streams** farm, high up on the slopes of Franschhoek Mountain. You can savour the

Haute Cabrière's cool mountainside restaurant and cellar, setting of gourmet cuisine matched with Cabrière wines.

salmon trout cooked a dozen ways in as many restaurants, and buy more to take home – raw, cold- or hot-smoked – for future feasts.

Down a leafy side street in the heart of the village is a unique combination of art gallery, antique shop, *fromagerie* and informal restaurant. Visitors to La Grange can taste and purchase more than 40 South African cheeses, including half a dozen that are made there, at **La Fromagerie**.

No gourmet capital worth its salt would be without a source of quality chocolate. Chocoholic heaven in Franschhoek is **Huguenot Fine Chocolates** on the main road, where two local lads, who trained in Belgium, whip up a tantalizing and irresistible selection of handmade truffles and silky-smooth bonbons.

For every item of valley produce, there's a fine wine just waiting to complement it.

RESTAURANTS IN THE 'GOURMET CAPITAL'

Connoisseurs of food and wine regard Franschhoek as one of South Africa's foremost gourmet destinations. The local chefs work hard to maintain this reputation, whether they are heading the kitchens of five-star

RANSCHHOEK

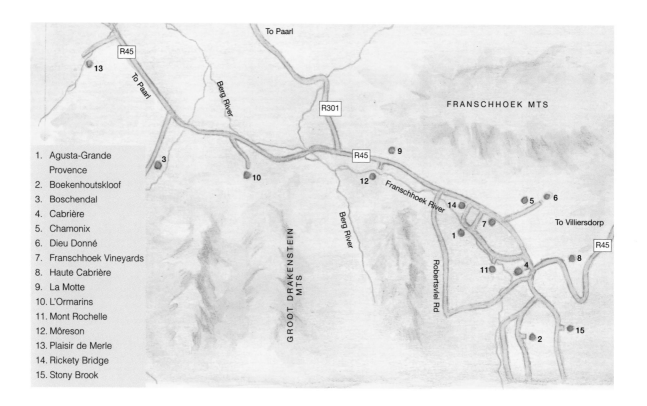

1. Agusta-Grande
   Provence
2. Boekenhoutskloof
3. Boschendal
4. Cabrière
5. Chamonix
6. Dieu Donné
7. Franschhoek Vineyards
8. Haute Cabrière
9. La Motte
10. L'Ormarins
11. Mont Rochelle
12. Môreson
13. Plaisir de Merle
14. Rickety Bridge
15. Stony Brook

restaurants or filling the need for coffee and cake. The village delis also pamper the palates of those looking for the makings of a portable feast.

Fierce competition helps to maintain high standards – with more than 40 eateries in town, there is no room for inferior fare.

On Môreson wine farm **Bread & Wine** restaurant specializes in homemade *charcuterie* and scrumptious breads to partner its robust reds.

Staying with informal venues, **Le Ballon Rouge** is a popular landmark, a pretty Victorian guesthouse that draws diners for meals that star valley ingredients. The wine list is also praiseworthy.

Right in the centre of the village is chef-patron Matthew Gordon's irresistible take on a classic village bistro. Dine on the stoep at **The French Connection** and watch the world go by.

At **Klein Oliphantshoek**, another tranquil guesthouse in a former mission station and school house, Camil Haas presents cuisine that is global, trendy and seasonal.

Talented chef and restaurateur Topsi Venter is a doyenne of good Cape food that maintains links with the Indonesian origins of Cape Malay cooking. **Topsi & Co** (the latter being her daughter and a parrot) occupy a former art gallery in the centre of town.

Le Quartier Français is an essential destination for gourmet visitors. This restaurant has featured in publications across the globe, and has garnered an impressive collection of awards. Book well ahead in season for either lunch or dinner.

Boschendal estate serves one of the most popular and generous buffet lunches in the Cape, for which visitors book up to six months ahead.

Another perennial favourite is **La Petite Ferme**, which clings to the slopes of the Franschhoek Pass and offers wraparound views of the valley. Its reputation for serving seasonal cuisine that is fresh, tasty and unpretentious endures: if popular items are removed from the menu, patrons demand their return.

Also on the pass is gastronomic gem **Haute Cabrière,** where the marriage of food and wine is taken to the ultimate. The restaurant and cellar is set into the mountainside, a rose-strewn bunker where half or full portions of chef Matthew Gordon's superb creations are matched to Cabrière wines from the cellar below.

A former parfumerie, transformed into a Mediterranean guesthouse, is also the home of **Monneaux** restaurant, where vibrant tastes of Africa, served in a tranquil courtyard, pleases all the senses.

L'Ormarins manor house boasts an imposing neo-classical gable.

Al fresco dining in a Gallic setting is on the menu at Le Quartier Français.

WINES OF THE FRANSCHHOEK VALLEY

It's more than fitting that this French corner of the Cape should produce superb sparkling wines from noble Champagne varieties using the mèthode champenoise.

In addition to these Cap Classiques, the small ward of Franschhoek has blossomed into producing a wide range of wines today, and that includes rewarding reds as well as notable whites. Wine lovers are able to taste a succession of excellent Sauvignon Blancs, Chardonnays and the trademark Semillons, a variety currently enjoying something of a revival.

There are about 25 wineries in the Franschhoek area, ranging from large historic estates to tiny wineries manned by former businessmen and the number increases annually.

The combination of scientific analyses and sophisticated techniques have seen the quality of both red and white wines soar in recent years. Franschhoek wines also benefit from the expertise and enthusiasm of the Vignerons de Franschhoek, a group of wine farmers who promote the valley and its products.

The following suggestions of wineries to visit and wines to taste are just a guide for those with limited time and knowledge of the area and include only wineries that are open to the public without prior appointment:

Sparkling wine: Cabrière wine estate. Saturday morning is show time, when exuberant proprietor and winemaker Baron Achim von Arnim leads the cellar tour.

Some producers of top white wines: Boschendal (Sauvignon Blanc and Chardonnay), Cape Chamonix (Chardonnay), L'Ormarins (Blanc Fumé), Mont Rochelle (Chardonnay), Môreson (Chardonnay), Plaisir de Merle (Chardonnay).

Some producers of top red wines: Boekenhoutskloof (Syrah and Cabernet Sauvignon), La Motte (Millennium and Shiraz), L'Ormarins (Optima), Môreson (Magia); Plaisir de Merle (Cabernet Sauvignon), Rickety Bridge (Cabernet Sauvignon and Shiraz), Stony Brook (Cabernet Sauvignon Reserve).

Historic and elegant venues include: Agusta-Grande Provence, Boschendal, La Motte, L'Ormarins, Plaisir de Merle.

Intimate boutique wineries include: Dieu Donné, Mont Rochelle, Rickety Bridge, Stony Brook.

Hospitable venues that cater for crowds include: Boschendal, Cape Chamonix, Franschhoek Vineyards, Môreson, all of which also operate restaurants, for which booking is essential at high season.

Country classics starring valley produce are the culinary hallmarks of La Petite Ferme.

MUST-SEE PLACES

The Huguenot Memorial and Museum, at the end of Huguenot Road, commemorate the arrival at the Cape of the French refugees at the close of the 17th century. The memorial enjoys a stunning setting at the foot of the Franschhoek Pass, in a garden featuring a riot of roses in the warmer months. The adjacent museum houses a wealth of Huguenot treasures, furniture and glassware, along with early letters and property deeds that attract many South Africans in search of their Gallic roots.

FRANSCHHOEK

DUNCAN'S SMOKED SALMON FISH TEA

This soup is a delight, not only for its wonderful flavours, but also for the odd expressions on diners' faces when a large, old-fashioned tea cup and saucer are placed in front of them. In the cup are several bits of seafood, roe and leaves. Tell diners not to eat these, says chef Duncan Docherty, as some people think it is sushi! Then the big teapot comes around … There can be no better way to recall the wonderful tastes and innovative spirit of fine fare from Franschhoek! This recipe feeds 12, but ingredients can be halved. You can make the stock the day before.

3 litres smoked salmon stock (see right)
6 small prawns, peeled and halved lengthways
6 scallops, halved
80 g smoked salmon trout, thinly sliced
80 g fresh salmon trout, thinly sliced
80 g fresh line fish, diced
saffron strands
bunch of fresh coriander
100 g salmon trout caviar
salt
pepper

SMOKED SALMON TROUT STOCK
500 g smoked salmon trout bones and trimmings
celery stalks, roughly chopped
2 large leeks, white part only, roughly chopped
1 large onion, roughly chopped
1 clove garlic, roughly chopped
2 large carrot, roughly chopped
250 ml (1 cup) dry white wine
sprigs of fresh tarragon and dill
3 litres fish stock (available in plastic sachets, from-supermarkets)

First make the stock. Rinse the salmon bones and trimmings and add to remaining stock ingredients in a large saucepan. Bring to a gentle simmer and simmer slowly for 3 hours; if you boil this stock it will turn cloudy and spoil the appearance of the 'tea'. After 3 hours, strain the stock through a fine strainer and then through muslin. It should be a clear pink, herby and well seasoned.

When you are ready to serve, place the following in the base of each of 12 large tea cups (or wide, old-fashioned soup plates): half a prawn, half a scallop, a few slices of smoked and fresh salmon trout, a few pieces of line fish, 3 strands saffron, 3 coriander leaves, and a few salmon eggs.

Bring the salmon stock to a boil and pour into a warmed teapot. Pour the hot stock into the tea cups, and the fish will cook in front of the diners' eyes.

Serves 12

THE FRENCH CONNECTION'S SMOKED DUCK SALAD WITH A RASPBERRY VERJUICE DRESSING

2 smoked duck breasts
salt and black pepper
250 g firm, dry feta cheese
flesh from ½ small, ripe watermelon
baby salad leaves
1 punnet alfalfa sprouts

DRESSING
2 punnets fresh raspberries
125 ml (½ cup) castor sugar
125 ml (½ cup) verjuice
125 ml (½ cup) water
200–250 ml (⅘–1 cup) extra-virgin olive oil

First make the dressing. Place the raspberries in a small saucepan, add the sugar, verjuice and water and bring to the boil. Reduce the heat and simmer for 5-8 minutes, then leave to cool. Purée the mixture and pass through a fine sieve. Return the sieved mixture to the blender then, with the motor running, add the olive oil, drop by drop.
When the mixture starts to emulsify, increase the pouring rate of the oil to a slow, thin stream.
Rub the fatty skin side of the duck with salt and pepper. Preheat a heavy-based frying pan, then add the duck breasts, skin side down, and sear over high heat for 2 minutes. Turn the duck breasts over and sear the other side for 2 minutes. Cool to room temperature.
Cut the feta cheese into strips and shave with a sharp vegetable peeler. Scoop out small balls of watermelon, using a melon baller. Cut the duck into 1–2 mm-thick slices.
To serve, arrange the baby salad leaves in the centre of a serving plate. Add half the duck slices and half the watermelon balls. Repeat this step, so that the dish acquires a little height. Sprinkle the shaved feta cheese over, drizzle with the dressing and garnish with the alfalfa sprouts.

Serves 4–6

HONEY LAVENDER ICE CREAM
WITH DAINTY BISCUITS

Camil Haas of Klein Oliphantshoek learnt to use only seasonal produce when he and his wife Ingrid lived in Turkey and in France. Now, he would not cook any other way. He says that the lavender grown in Franschhoek is more profuse, with a more intense perfume than that found in Provence. Camil recommends whipping the cream for this ice cream by hand rather than using a machine.

ICE CREAM	DAINTY BISCUITS
500 ml (2 cups) milk	90 g icing sugar
60 ml (4 tbsp) white sugar	100 ml (6½ tbsp) cake flour
a handful of chopped lavender tops	4 egg whites (from large eggs)
40 ml (2 heaped tbsp) honey	25 ml (5 tsp) butter, melted
500 ml (2 cups) fresh cream	a pinch of salt
60 ml (4 tbsp) white sugar	
5 egg yolks	seasonal berries or sliced fruit
100 g white sugar	honey
	fresh mint sprigs or lavender

To make the ice cream, combine the milk, 60 ml (4 tbsp) sugar, lavender and honey in a pan, and bring to simmering point. Remove and leave for 20 minutes. Whip the cream and 60 ml (4 tbsp) sugar together until soft peaks form, then chill. Whisk the egg yolks and 100 g sugar lightly. Strain the lavender mixture, stir in the egg yolks and simmer until thickened. Cool, then whip in the cream and place the bowl in ice-cold water. Transfer to the freezer and stir a few times while freezing to break up any crystals.

To make the biscuits, combine all the ingredients to make a soft dough. Chill until ready to bake. Line a greased baking sheet with baking parchment, drop tablespoonfuls of dough on to the sheet and shape into 2-mm-thick rounds. Bake at 200 °C for about 8 minutes. Transfer very carefully to a wire rack. To serve, place a few berries on each plate and drizzle with honey. Place a biscuit in the centre of each plate, top with a scoop of ice cream, another biscuit and a second scoop of ice cream. Garnish with a sprig of mint or lavender and serve immediately.

Makes 30–35 biscuits

GORGONZOLA CUSTARD
WITH PICKLED FENNEL AND TOMATO CONFIT

Margot Janse is the talented executive chef of Le Quartier Français, a restaurant that has been voted as one of the top 50 restaurants in the world. She offers an innovative selection of cheese-based dishes as alternatives to a cheese board. This is one of the best.

CUSTARD
190 ml (¾ cup) cream
190 ml (¾ cup) milk
200 g Gorgonzola or local blue cheese, crumbled
3 large eggs
2 large egg yolks

PICKLED FENNEL
250 ml (1 cup) white-wine vinegar
250 ml (1 cup) white sugar
250 ml (1 cup) water
5 ml (1 tsp) fennel seeds
5 ml (1 tsp) black peppercorns
4 fennel bulbs, thinly sliced

TOMATO CONFIT
6 plum (jam) tomatoes, skinned, seeded and halved
1 clove garlic, peeled and sliced
1 sprig thyme
30 ml (2 tbsp) olive oil
salt and pepper

Make the custard a day ahead of serving. Preheat the oven to 150 °C. Place the cream, milk and cheese in a saucepan and bring to simmering point, cooking until the cheese has melted. Cool. Whisk the eggs and egg yolks together and stir in the cooled cream. Divide the mixture among 6 small ovenproof ramekins and place in a bain-marie filled with enough warm water to come two-thirds up the sides of the ramekins. Bake until set, about 25 minutes. Leave to cool in the water bath.

For the pickled fennel, bring all the ingredients, except the fennel, to the boil. Cool. Add the fennel slices, then marinate for 24 hours. To make the tomato confit, preheat the oven to 100 °C. Toss the halved tomatoes with all the other ingredients. Place on a baking sheet in the oven and leave to dry for 1½ hours. When ready to serve, unmould the custards onto plates, surround with fennel and tomato and drizzle the fennel pickling liquid over.

Serves 6

CEMAGTIG OM WYN
TE VERKOOP- OF VAN
DIE HAND TE SIT

AUTHORIZED TO SELL
WINE - OR TO
DISPOSE OF IT

1

2

3

OVERBERG

The last glimpse of False Bay, shining far below, makes a memorable picture as travellers reach the summit of Sir Lowry's Pass. Over the top, a new world unfolds as you descend into the high-land bowl of Elgin. Mountain slopes thick with fynbos are interspersed with timber forests, while orchards of apple and pear trees march over hills bisected by a multitude of streams.

ABOVE   *The Hamilton Russell production cellar.*

OPPOSITE   *Old basket press at Beaumont Wines (1); Bouchard-Finlayson (2); Walker Bay Wines (3); grainlands near Caledon (4).*

This is the gateway to the Overberg, a region so rich in resources that a stream of pioneers struggled up the steep slopes of the old Gantouw Pass with wagons and teams of oxen in order to reach its treasures.

Whether you arrive in spring, when the orchards are a sea of blossom, or in summer, when the trees are in verdant dress, the scene is splendid. Early autumn sees boughs heavy with fruit, while bare trees outlined against a snow-clad mountain backdrop present a wintry picture of stark beauty.

Visitors with time to linger can visit fruit and flower farms along the mountain highways that make up the Four Passes and Fruit Routes.

Beyond Elgin lies Bot River and a gentler pass, whose southerly slopes lead to the coastline of Walker Bay, where pounding surf, pristine white beaches, and excellent angling lure travellers off the national road.

The most famous of the coastal resorts is undoubtedly Hermanus, renowned as one of the best whale-watching destinations in the world. It's also a lodestar for hikers and nature lovers, as it offers cliff walks and trails through magnificent nature reserves.

The N2 continues to follow the Great Wagon Road of the 18th century, swinging east to the ridges of the Rûens, where wheatfields and pastures offer a kaleidoscope of gold and green and the blue crane – South Africa's national bird – walks tall.

You will have to work a little harder here to hunt down superb wines at boutique wineries tucked away from view. But the rewards will be overwhelming, and

The Bouchard-Finlayson winery sprawls below the Raed-na-Gael ridge where it is home to aristocratic wines.

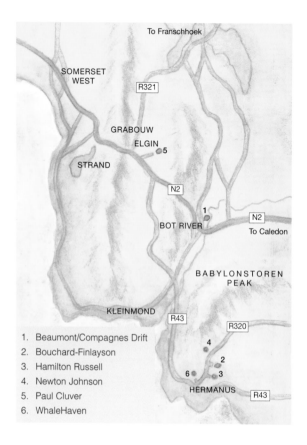

1. Beaumont/Compagnes Drift
2. Bouchard-Finlayson
3. Hamilton Russell
4. Newton Johnson
5. Paul Cluver
6. WhaleHaven

will perfectly complement the culinary bounty of this partly tamed paradise.

OVERBERG PRODUCE AND CUISINE

Elgin is apple country – with pears, peaches and nectarines vying for second place.

Apples are available fresh and dried, puréed and juiced, and transformed into delicious ciders. Along with filling innumerable pie shells, apples and pears feature in a treasure chest of dishes, both sweet and savoury, created and collected by valley cooks over the years. A good place to sample these is the trio of excellent farmstalls along the national road. **The Orchard** is followed by **Peregrine** and **Houw Hoek**, all of which offer fresh produce and deli items, bakes and preserves, and serve breakfasts, teas and lunches of consistently good quality.

The Caledon Globe onion, well known for its exceptional keeping qualities, is cultivated from Botrivier through to Caledon, where wheat and sheep take precedence on many Overberg farms.

Traditional fare based on lamb, wheat and game birds such as guinea fowl can be found at the **Dassiesfontein** farmstall outside Caledon. Ask the knowledgeable staff of the Caledon Museum for other sources of home-cooked feasts and stock up on confectionery and preserves while you are there.

At the coastal resorts, the line fish reigns supreme. Depending on the season, it could be Cape salmon or kabeljou (kob), yellowtail or a less common species – all are delectable simply grilled or pan fried. Abalone, or perlemoen as it is called here, was once plentiful but is now both scarce and prohibitively expensive.

Mountain and farm cheeses are produced by **Vogelvallei** farm at Botrivier and the **Camphill Farm** community near Hermanus.

The little village of Stanford is home to a couple of quaint restaurants with a reputation for great food.

The youngberries grown at Swellendam – an attractive and historic town off the N2, which boasts several good restaurants – also star in a delicious liqueur.

For gourmet fare head for Hermanus and the luxurious Marine Hotel, one of three hotels comprising the Liz McGrath Collection. Operating serenely from its clifftop setting, the hotel houses two attractive restaurants.. The elegant **Pavilion** restaurant presents a

contemporary menu. while **Seafood at the Marine** is the self-explanatory name of the second. The town is also home to several casual restaurants, some with sea views, that serve fresh and fishy fare.

On the Arabella Country Estate near Kleinmond, the Western Cape Hotel and Spa houses the **Premiere** restaurant, which serves epicurean dinners of international standard, with service to match.

WINES OF THE OVERBERG

The Overberg wine district encompasses the wards of Elgin and Walker Bay. A new viticultural area east of

Dining at the Marine Hotel's Pavilion restaurant can be an intimate affair.

Vines on De Rust farm in Elgin, source of the stylish Paul Cluver wines.

Caledon in the direction of Cape Agulhas may develop to be a third in this diverse area.

Both Elgin and Walker Bay are prime quality, cool-climate sites, with the vineyards of Walker Bay, in particular, benefiting from the maritime climate.

De Rust is one of the oldest and largest estates in Elgin. While deciduous fruit is still produced there, the Cluver family started planting vines more than 20 years ago. Today **Paul Cluver** wines are highly rated both in the UK and locally, along with **Thandi** wines, which are produced in the same cellar by former labourers in one of South Africa's most successful empowerment initiatives. The estate hosts summer entertainment at its outdoor forest amphitheatre too.

At Botrivier, take time to visit **Beaumont**, another family venue with more than wine on the menu. At this former outpost of the Dutch East India Company, both reds and whites of quality are made, jewellery and art

are displayed on open days and charming self-catering cottages entice you to linger overnight.

At Walker Bay, you should start your wine tasting at the site on the slopes of the Hemel-en-Aarde valley, where Tim Hamilton Russell pioneered his wines. Today **Hamilton Russell Vineyards** focus on the Burgundian classics, Pinot Noir and Chardonnay, both of which receive star ratings by top writers and judges on several continents and command high prices.

More excellent Pinot Noir and a choice of Chardonnays await visitors at **Bouchard-Finlayson**, vanguard of Franco-South African vinous ventures, which also offers Sauvignon Blanc, another Hemel-en-Aarde speciality.

Try **Newton Johnson's** accessible wines or head for the well-named **WhaleHaven**, not only for its proximity to the giant sea mammals, but for its cosy tasting area, firelit in winter. Here Storm Kreusch combines motherhood with winemaking with consummate skill. The aristocrats, Pinot Noir and Chardonnay, are complemented by Merlot and Cabernet Sauvignon.

In the near future, tasting itineraries are likely to extend to areas not yet known for wine production. Meanwhile, if time is short, head to **Wine Village**, a Hemel-en-Aarde outlet that stocks the best of Walker Bay, along with the Hermanus Heritage Collection. Look out, too, for **Wine & Company**, a Hermanus shop worth a visit, if only to taste Bartho Eksteen's Sauvignon Blanc.

MUST-SEE PLACES

Cape Agulhas, Africa's most southerly point, is simply marked with an inscribed plinth. Nearby stands the second-oldest working lighthouse in the country, which also houses Africa's only lighthouse museum.

The entire village of **Kassiesbaai**, at Arniston, has been declared a national monument. This tiny fishing village is still inhabited by families who wrest a precarious living from the sea, but the women also produce fine craftwork and will present delicious teas and light meals, if given notice.

The oldest mission station in South Africa is to be found six kilometres from Greyton. **Genadendal** was established in 1738 and today the Moravian church, mission museum, Old Print Shop and water mill are historic village treasures.

OVERBERG

DUO OF YELLOWTAIL AND TIGER PRAWNS WITH MASCARPONE AND WARM BEAN SPROUT SALAD

Louis van Reenen, the executive chef of the historic Marine Hotel in Hermanus, is a talented and passionate South African chef who admires the simplicity of good, contemporary British cuisine. In this recipe he uses yellowtail, a delectable game fish found along the Cape coast in summer.

2 fresh yellowtail steaks or fillets, each 160−180 g	**SALAD**
salt and white pepper	20 ml (4 tsp) olive oil
6 tiger prawns, deveined and shelled,	2 carrots, peeled and cut into julienne strips
except for tail sections	2 leeks, trimmed and cut into julienne strips
fresh lemon juice	2 onions, peeled and cut into strips
20 ml (4 tsp) olive oil	45 ml (3 tbsp) bean sprouts
30 ml (2 tbsp) mascarpone cheese	20 ml (4 tsp) sesame oil
30 ml (2 tbsp) chopped chives	10 ml (2 tsp) soy sauce
lemon juice	10 g flaked almonds
2 lemon wedges	salt and white pepper

First make the salad. Heat the olive oil and sauté the carrots, leeks and onions together until just tender, then add the bean sprouts, sesame oil, soy sauce and flaked almonds. Season the mixture and keep it warm.

Preheat the oven to 180 °C. Wipe the fish and season with salt and pepper. Seal the fish on both sides in a hot frying pan, then transfer to an ovenproof dish and roast for 6−8 minutes.

Meanwhile, season the prawns with salt and pepper and toss in a little lemon juice.

Heat the oil in a non-stick frying pan and cook the prawns until firm and pink.

Mix the mascarpone cheese with the chives and season with salt and lemon juice to taste.

To serve, divide the salad between two warmed plates, placing it in the centre. Top each with fish.

Arrange the prawns around the fish, then top each fish portion with a spoonful of mascarpone mixture.

Garnish each with a lemon wedge.

Serves 2

ELGIN FARMSTALL SPECIAL APPLE CAKE

CAKE	FILLING
500 g cake flour	100 g butter
250 g sugar	250 g sugar
10 ml (2 tsp) baking powder	pinch of salt
pinch of salt	12 cooking apples, peeled, cored and sliced
250 g butter at room temperature	juice of 2 lemons, or to taste
4 egg yolks	2 ml (½ tsp) ground cloves
	5 ml (1 tsp) ground cinnamon
	125 ml (½ cup) sultanas (optional)
	60 ml (4 tbsp) cornflour
	60 ml (4 tbsp) cold water

Preheat the oven to 180 °C.

For the cake batter, combine the flour, sugar, baking powder and salt. Rub in the butter with your fingertips until the mixture resembles fine crumbs. Beat the egg yolks lightly and mix into the batter.

Leave to rest while making the filling.

To make the filling, melt the butter, add the sugar and stir until dissolved. Add the salt, apples, lemon juice, cloves, cinnamon and sultanas, if using, and cook the mixture gently until the apples are just tender. Do not overcook.

Mix the cornflour and water to a paste, and stir in enough to thicken the apple mixture.

To assemble the cake, oil the sides of a 7-cm-deep, 28-cm-diametre round, loose-based or spring-form cake pan. Press about two-thirds of the batter onto the base and up the sides of the pan.

Spoon in the apple filling, then cover with the remaining cake batter.

Bake for about 45 minutes. Leave to cool completely − preferably overnight − before slicing.

Makes 1 x 28 cm cake

WORCESTER

There is so much to discover in this huge valley, ringed by impossibly blue mountains, that locals maintain it can take a lifetime to unearth its multi-layered charms. Yet, for many travellers, Worcester is little more than a petrol stop on the great north road from Cape Town to the Karoo and beyond.

ABOVE *Colombard, used for brandy production as well as wine.*

OPPOSITE *The Keerom mountians and Nuy vineyards (1); farmstall near Overhex (2); Colombard vineleaf (3); spraying the muscadel vines at Nuy (4).*

Those who pause awhile will find vineyards and orchards that give way to indigenous flora on the mountain slopes. Towering cliffs make vertical paths for waterfalls, which multiply as snow caps the peaks of the Du Toitskloof and Hex River Mountains.

The valley is bisected by the Breede River that has forced a route down Michell's Pass in the Ceres mountains, to flow across the broad valley, which has Worcester as its principal town.

Soon after the town was founded in 1820, several beautiful buildings arose, a few of which survive today. Among these is the farmstead that now houses the Kleinplasie Living Open-air Museum, where traditional industries like making candles, baking bread, milling wheat and forging iron are carried out in the farmyard.

During the dry, cold winter, aloes and bulbous plants bloom to add shafts of colour to the vegetation in the world-renowned Karoo National Botanical Gardens outside the town, a precursor to the glorious display of spring flowers from August to September.

PRODUCE AND CUISINE

The food and wine of the Worcester region share certain characteristics with those of many of the inhabitants: down-to-earth, hospitable, generous but unpretentious.

There is a wine house next to the **Kleinplasie** museum that stocks a wide range of the affordable wines made in this extended district. In the adjoining restaurant, hungry visitors can tuck into hearty servings of well-cooked traditional and contemporary food, without any frills, provided no functions are in progress.

Heritage farm fare also features on the menu of the restaurant at the **Nuy Valley Guest House**, near the Nuy winery off the R60.

Farmstalls feature alongside major and minor roads. They stock table grapes of good quality from January through to May, as well as other seasonal fruit and vegetables. Some stalls sell good preserves and farm

Worcester vineyards in the Breede River valley are irrigated from Lake Marais at Brandvlei.

bread, while the one on the R60 between Worcester and Overhex is renowned for its huge variety of gourds, artistically piled around an old tree outside the shop. Every type of squash and pumpkin is sold at give-away prices.

Deciduous fruit, sweet melons and grapes make other summer bargain buys.

WINE IN THE WORCESTER VALLEY

As with other commodities, so with wine: there's a fair amount of snob value attached to certain areas and particular labels. This is reflected among those wine lovers who stay on the Cape Town side of the mountain for their table wines, regarding Worcester as good only for the fortified product.

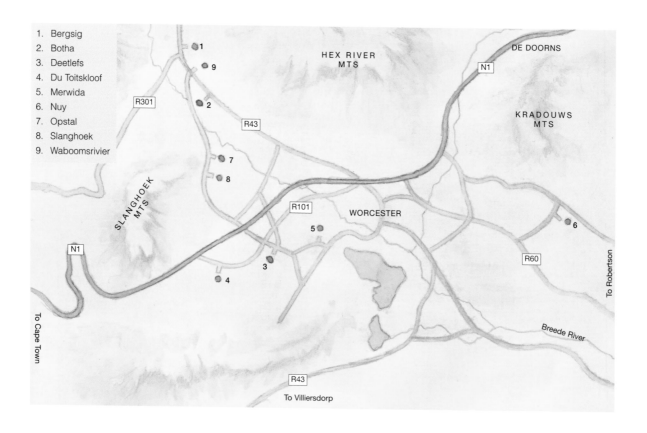

1. Bergsig
2. Botha
3. Deetlefs
4. Du Toitskloof
5. Merwida
6. Nuy
7. Opstal
8. Slanghoek
9. Waboomsrivier

Meanwhile, canny consumers with more adventurous palates take the byways to secluded valleys such as Slanghoek, head north towards Wolseley, and southeast to Nuy, to stock up on good wines at even better prices.

The Worcester winelands account for 20 per cent of South Africa's wine grape crop, making it the largest, in terms of volume, in South Africa. Chenin blanc has always been the backbone cultivar here, grown both for brandy distilling and, more recently, for grape juice and concentrate.

The last decade of the 20th century saw many changes, as a new generation of enthusiastic vintners decided that they were not going to miss out on the recently opened export market.

They looked beyond Chenin to Chardonnay and Sauvignon Blanc, and then focused on the fashionable reds, finding suitable areas to plant Cabernet Sauvignon and Shiraz, along with some Merlot and Pinotage.

Cellars were upgraded and some co-ops brought in consultants from overseas, resulting in an extraordinary mixture of accented English, the common language of communication.

The new millennium was celebrated with promising results and burgeoning export orders.

BRANDY

Brandy is widely regarded as South Africa's national spirit, accounting for some 55 percent of spirits consumed in this country. Although South Africa is only the sixth largest producer in the world, it boasts the biggest brandy production facility, the **KWV International** brandy cellar, situated on the outskirts of Worcester (see page 105). Even visitors with little interest in the spirit are bowled over by the sheer size of the operation, with its 120 traditional brandy pot stills, two large French alembic stills and two enormous continuous stills.

Brandy has been distilled in South Africa since 1672, although the 'fire water' produced by a Dutch East India Company ship's cook in 1672 was a far cry from the smooth, sophisticated drink of today.

Quality started to improve about 100 years later, but it was only after 1825 that standards rose with the establishment of well-known Cape companies like Van Ryn and Collis, the Castle Wine and Brandy Company and EK Green.

This was further boosted by the efforts of distiller René Santhagen, a French officer who moved on to the farm Oude Molen near Stellenbosch with his cognac stills in 1903.

In 1918 South Africa's brandy industry suffered a setback because of overproduction, but the establishment of the KWV helped to check the surplus through legislation and quality controls.

The South African Brandy Foundation was established in 1984, and today its members are responsible for nearly all the brandy production in this country. The standard has improved to the extent that the Cape produces some excellent brandies, which have won accolades in Europe and attracted some famous Old World brandy makers south to the Cape.

Since 1993, when estate brandies became an official term under the Wine of Origin scheme, boutique distilleries have proliferated at wineries in Paarl and Wellington, Stellenbosch and the Little Karoo, among other regions. Distinguished pot-still brandies are being produced, while a few independent blenders are adding to the range with products that are intriguing certain European connoisseurs.

WHERE TO GO, WHAT TO TASTE

A map of the Worcester Wine Route reveals that tasting sorties can take place to the north and south of the town, as well as to the east and west.

For those who have limited time and cannot meander back and forth, here are a few guidelines geared to the compass points, and using the town of Worcester as base camp.

Just a few of the 23 co-ops and the handful of estates have been included, all of them open for tastings and sales without appointment. If you have time to visit more of them, you will be assured of a warm welcome, along with easy-drinking wines at pleasing prices.

TO THE SOUTHWEST

Heading south from Worcester on the N1, take the left-hand turnoff to the R101 and drive towards Rawsonville. Beyond the village, on the Cape Town side, you will find **Du Toitskloof Winery**, which boasts a large band of devoted customers. The wide range of easy-drinking whites – the crisp Sauvignon Blanc in particular – is as popular as the award-winning, budget-priced Hanepoot Jerepigo, while dry reds have recently extended the choice from this go-ahead team.

The entrance to the **Deetlefs** estate is in the village of Rawsonville. Semillon is the speciality of sixth-

Nuy Co-op sells excellent muscadels at giveaway prices.

Slanghoek Winery recently celebrated its 50th anniversary with a clutch of awards for its products. Highly rated are both the red Muscadel Jerepigo and the ruby Port, but sample the Sauvignon Blanc and Chardonnay/Sauvignon Blanc blend as well.

Even further up the valley is **Opstal,** a pretty estate that draws customers for a couple of good red wines, and sociable evenings that begin with a 'haunted cellar tour' and finish with a 'medieval banquet'.

NORTH OF WORCESTER

Leaving Worcester on the N1, take the R43 which heads north towards Wolseley and Ceres. On the way is the **Botha Wine Cellar**, a co-op that offers bargain-priced reds that include a good Cabernet Sauvignon. They also make an enjoyable Colombard and good Jerepigos.

Waboomsrivier is another co-op that has recently celebrated 50 years of winemaking with a switch in focus from white to red wines, and with ruby Cabernet receiving special attention. Bottles sport the Wagenboom label.

Further up the road lies the **Bergsig** estate, a venerable farm that has been selling bulk wine since 1843. New directions here see some wine going overseas, and a good deal being produced for local supermarkets. Visitors will find a good range of red and white wines.

TO THE SOUTHEAST

Leave Worcester on the R60, the well-travelled road to Robertson, and look out for Nuy farm and winestall, just before the turnoff to the **Nuy** winery. It nestles in a hidden valley, both remote and deeply rural, where veteran winemaker Wilhelm Linde continues to make magnificent muscadel − selling at unbelievable prices − and delicate white wines that delight legions of fans.

generation winemaker Kobus Deetlefs, but his Chenin Blanc is not run-of-the-mill, and his Pinotage is one of the best in the area.

Leaving Rawsonville on the R101 you will pass several co-ops, of which **Merwida Co-op** is probably the largest and best known. The range of popular whites has been extended, while investment in red cultivars has produced a good ruby Cabernet and Cabernet Sauvignon/Merlot blend.

TO THE NORTHWEST

From the R101, take the right-hand turnoff signposted 'Goudini Spa' and 'Slanghoek'. The latter is a green belt that slithers along the Worcester side of the Du Toitskloof and Bains Kloof mountains, all the way to the Breede River. It's a place of sweet seclusion, where comparatively few travellers venture.

THE BRANDY ROUTE

Van Ryn cellar at Vlottenburg (below) – which offers visitors views of the distillation process, along with the vast maturation cellars and a demonstration of barrel-making by coopers – makes a logical start, while Avontuur estate, Louiesenhof and Uitkyk are other stops in the Stellenbosch region. Backsberg and Laborie in Paarl and Cabrière in Franschhoek are also on the Boland route.

The second section follows Route 62, through the Little Karoo, from the huge KWV brandy cellar at Worcester to the museum at Montagu, then on to the Barrydale Cellars for a tasting of Joseph Barry brandy.

Calitzdorp is the next town on the route; while more famous for Port, top estate Boplaas has a long tradition of brandy distilling as well.

At Oudtshoorn, Grundheim farm, well known for its fruity liqueurs, launched its maiden vintage pot-still brandy in 2002. The Kango Co-op makes afford-able brandies, among which their hanepoot brandy is particularly popular. Finally, between Oudtshoorn and De Rust, the delightful estate of Mons Ruber has revived its early distilling practices and now makes estate brandy, distilling the spirit over an open fire in a venerable still surrounded by the startling red cliffs after which the estate is named.

KAAPSCHE JONGENS

bunches of firm ripe grapes, preferably hanepoot

SYRUP
250 ml (1 cup) white sugar
250 ml (1 cup) water
375 ml (1½ cups) South Africa brandy

After washing the bunches, remove the grapes from the stems, leaving a small stalk attached to each. Prick each grape with a sterilized needle.

To make the syrup, combine the sugar and water and bring to the boil, then cook briefly until the liquid starts to look syrupy.

Remove from the stove and stir in the brandy. Pack the grapes into warm sterilized jars and top up with the syrup. Screw the lids on loosely, then sterilize the jars in a water bath, on top of the stove. Seal tightly and leave for a couple of months before using.

BRANDY TRUFFLES

300 g dark chocolate
250 g unsalted butter
550 g icing sugar, sifted
45 ml (3 tbsp) South African brandy
chocolate vermicelli or cocoa powder

Melt the chocolate over simmering water on top of the
stove, or at 50 per cent power in a microwave oven.
Cream the butter and sugar until light and fluffy.
Add the melted chocolate to the butter mixture. Beat
well, then mix in the brandy. Cool the mixture a little,
then scoop out teaspoonfuls and roll it into little balls.
Roll the balls in chocolate vermicilli or cocoa powder.
Chill until required.

Makes about 50 truffles

MALVA PUDDING

This is one of the outstanding favourites among traditional Cape puddings, a warm, comforting finale on a chilly evening. Although several regions will lay claim to it, Worcester cooks say that versions of this dessert first originated in their part of the Boland, and newer versions were called Telephone Pudding because, when the telephone reached the farms, it was passed on to new cooks over the phone.

2 eggs, at room temperature
250 ml (1 cup) castor sugar
15 ml (1 tbsp) smooth apricot jam
310 ml (1 cup plus 4 tbsp) cake flour
5 ml (1 tsp) bicarbonate of soda
pinch of salt
30 ml (2 tbsp) butter
125 ml (½ cup) milk
5 ml (1 tsp) vinegar

SAUCE
250 ml (1 cup) cream
100 g butter
125 ml (½ cup) sugar
125 ml (½ cup) brandy

Preheat the oven to 180 °C.
Beat the eggs and castor sugar together until light and fluffy. Add the apricot jam and mix well. Sift the flour, bicarbonate of soda and salt. Melt the butter and add to the milk. Add the vinegar. Fold the flour mixture into the egg mixture, alternating with the milk mixture. Spoon the batter into a greased ovenproof dish and bake for 45 minutes.
Combine all the sauce ingredients and bring to simmering point. When the pudding is removed from the oven, prick the top in several places, using a sharp knife, then pour the hot sauce over.
This pudding is excellent on its own, but it can also be served with warm custard, if desired.

Serves 6–8

ROBERTSON

ABOVE *Hospitable Van Loveren.*

OPPOSITE *Graham Beck Wines (1 & 2);*
Bon Courage maturation cellar (3); Branewynsdraai
restaurant and wine shop (4); keeping it cool (5);
Cape Dutch elegance at Bon Courage (6).

This beguiling valley is renowned for its delicious wine, magnificent roses and superior stud farms. To these attractions I would add warm hospitality, champagne air and value for money, all compelling reasons for planning a leisurely visit.

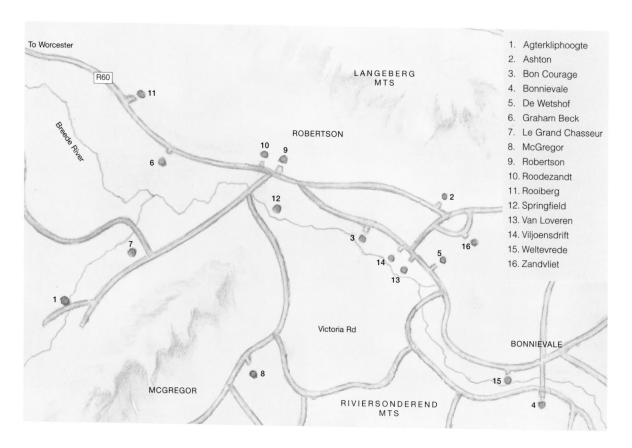

To Worcester

R60

LANGEBERG
MTS

Breede River

ROBERTSON

11

10 9

6

12

2

7

3

14

16

5

13

1

Victoria Rd

BONNIEVALE

8

15

MCGREGOR

RIVIERSONDEREND
MTS

4

1. Agterkliphoogte
2. Ashton
3. Bon Courage
4. Bonnievale
5. De Wetshof
6. Graham Beck
7. Le Grand Chasseur
8. McGregor
9. Robertson
10. Roodezandt
11. Rooiberg
12. Springfield
13. Van Loveren
14. Viljoensdrift
15. Weltevrede
16. Zandvliet

Part of the valley's appeal lies, I think, in its unique position, bridging the gap between the verdant and populous Boland and the semidesert terrain of the comparatively isolated Karoo. At this end of the Breede River valley the pace is slower, the lifestyle laid back and the climate delightful, apart from a handful of very hot days during late summer.

Villages known as havens of tranquillity often conceal hives of activity, as they are home to artists and potters, craftsman, healers and professionals who have fled the city. In addition to B&Bs, accommodation is offered at country inns, guesthouses, farm cottages and retreats.

Leaving the Worcester region by the R60, travellers whizz eastwards along a new newly widened highway, through pastures and vineyards interspersed with indigenous scrub that is transformed by spring flowers into stretches of blazing colour.

Well before the road dips toward Robertson, Rooiberg winery looms large, to be followed by ultramodern cellars, colourful reminders that both budget wines and those of the finest quality are on tap, side by side, throughout this valley.

Robertson is small enough to retain its rural charm, large enough to offer most services and amenities. More

Cape
FLAVOUR

wineries line one side of the R60, as it skirts the edge of the town. On the other side a bridge over the railway tracks leads to another, crossing the Breede River. This is followed by a fork, one arm leading to little-known wineries that beg to be explored, the other to McGregor, a bewitching village known to lure strangers back, time and again, until they succumb and stay forever …

Set amid rolling hills with a backdrop of the Langeberg mountains to the north and the Riviersonderend mountains to the south, the village was saved from through traffic and development after a planned mountain pass did not materialize. Today its claim to fame is as the best preserved example of a mid-19th century townscape. A meander along lanes boasting thatched cottages and apricot orchards presents enchanting Cape vernacular architecture in a setting of timeless tranquillity.

A branch road from the R60 follows the Breede River to Bonnievale, another hospitable and peaceful village, that boasts its fair share of cellars and guesthouses, along with a cheese factory.

Where this wineland loop rejoins the R60 it leads to Ashton, a major fruit-processing centre.

Hikers are well catered for in this region, while less strenuous attractions include gentle cruises down the Breede River, with wine tasting aboard.

The Old Mill Lodge dreams on at McGregor, offering visitors a rustic retreat and an ideal base for tasting expeditions.

ROBERTSON

PRODUCE AND CUISINE

Visitors arriving in the valley during November and December will find apricot orchards with boughs bent down to the earth, heavy with golden, perfumed fruit. Collect a bag or two from roadside farmstalls, or inquire about picking your own apricots from backyard orchards in village gardens, which may also yield salad greens.

Hard on their heels come juicy, sun-kissed peaches, which inspire a second burst of activity as crop surpluses are dried or bottled, or cooked into chunky jam and chutney for year-round reminders of summer.

The silvery foliage of sturdy young olive trees shimmers in the hills around McGregor. This biblical fruit is on sale at **Villagers**, the local coffee shop and craft centre, where you will find black, green and semi-dried olives and oil.

Branewynsdraai restaurant on the outskirts of Robertson offers contemporary and traditional South African classics, best savoured on the lawn under ancient pepper trees. Wines from every producer in the valley are stocked here.

For delectable light fare at pleasing prices, pop in to **Café Rosa**, which nestles in the green oasis of the well-stocked Robertson nursery.

In McGregor, the **Old Mill Lodge** is one of several options that prides itself on a good table – here the seasons dictate many of the ingredients for à la carte luncheons and three-course dinners, complemented by an award-winning winelist.

On the R60 between Robertson and Ashton, **Fraai Uitzicht 1798**, a working wine farm and guesthouse, also houses a good restaurant that presents contemporary fare starring home-grown produce.

A handful of valley wineries also offer refreshments ranging from snacks to coffee-shop fare, and several farmstalls cater for customers who want to linger awhile.

WHERE TO GO, WHAT TO TASTE

Few cellars in this valley are not worth a visit; in fact, many of them are good sources of affordable and dependable wines, while others offer superior products at competitive prices. It is easy to find a valley wine to complement your choice of food, be it a carnivorous feast or a dainty designer salad. Of the 30 producers, nearly all welcome the public without appointment.

Van Loveren Winery is as renowned for its lush gardens as it is for its wide range of well-priced wines.

Historic homestead at Zandvliet wine estate and stud farm.

The Robertson valley used to be known for quaffable whites and good, fortified Muscats, both red and white. Chenin Blanc and Colombard were the most popular cultivars and today delicious fruity wines are still made from these tolerant, undemanding grapes. They are often guava-scented, can be dry or off-dry, and are sold at bargain prices.

Toward the end of the 20th century, Chardonnay, Riesling, Sauvignon Blanc and Gewürztraminer started to supplant the older workhorse varieties. This investment was followed by a leap in quality that has placed Robertson on the map as a producer of fine whites from classic grapes, including Sauvignon Blanc.

The move towards red came next, with scientific matching of cultivar to suitable site preceding wide-spread planting. The early releases have shown that Shiraz, Cabernet Sauvignon, Merlot, Pinotage and ruby Cabernet can be grown successfully and transformed into red wines of great promise.

Here are a few guidelines for planning wine-tasting excursions in the BAR (Bonnievale, Ashton, Robertson) valley:

Producers of excellent sparkling wine: **Graham Beck Wines** is the undisputed star, producing successive vintages of superb Cap Classiques. The winery is widely regarded as one of the four most exciting in South Africa.

Some producers of excellent white wines: Many of the wines in the extensive **Bon Courage** range attract awards year after year.

At **De Wetshof**, back in the 1980s, Danie de Wet's pioneering work saw his 1985 Chardonnay being judged as the world's best at France's Vinexpo. Today, half a dozen superb Chardonnays can be tasted at the cellars, along with other whites.

On the **Springfield** estate, also regarded as being one of the four most exciting wineries in South Africa, dedicated and adventurous winemaker Abrie Bruwer produces outstanding Chardonnays and Sauvignon Blancs.

Van Loveren is a delightful farm to visit, with its riverside garden planted with a wide variety of trees. Good whites and white blends include those made from less common cultivars such as Pinot Gris and Fernão Pires.

Weltevrede Estate is another hospitable venue, which has a restaurant that offers traditional lunches. Along with an excellent Chardonnay and other good whites, they also offer a second, value-for-money range.

At **Zandvliet Estate** (and stud farm), a child-friendly venue, don't miss a taste of the Equus Chardonnay.

Some producers of very good red wines: **Bon Courage** is producing a promising Shiraz, and The Ridge Shiraz from **Graham Beck** is a single vineyard winner to be followed by exciting, exotic reds to come.

At **Springfield**, the Whole Berry Cabernet Sauvignon adds lustre to the valley's red reputation, while **Van Loveren** is making the whole gamut of reds.

Taste **Viljoensdrift**'s Shiraz and Cabernet Sauvignon while on a river cruise, and sip Shiraz and a scintillating blend of Cabernet, Merlot and Shiraz at **Zandvliet**.

Some producers of value-for-money wines of consistent quality: **Agterkliphoogte Co-op** (a budget-priced range bearing the Wandsbeck label); **Ashton Winery**, **Bonnievale Kelder**, **Le Grand Chasseur**, **McGregor Winery** (delicious whites and easy-drinking reds), **Robertson Winery** (in spite of huge volumes produced, high standards are maintained for both their Wide River and regular labels), **Roodezandt** (their white Muscadel is renowned), **Rooiberg Winery** (wide range, including an excellent red Muscadel).

MUST-SEE PLACES

Open Africa is a visionary project aimed at achieving sustainable, ecological, economic and social development across the continent, using our cultural, natural and wildlife heritage.

This non-profit foundation, funded largely by big business, enjoys input from prominent South Africans, including former president Nelson Mandela, who is its patron.

Afrikatourism, the practical arm of the project, aims to link the splendours of Africa through a continuous network of tourism routes from Cape to Cairo. Fynbos, whale-watching, diving, walking and historic routes are among those up on the website and attracting many visitors.

The **Cape Cuisine Route** tells diners where to find authentic tastes of Cape Malay delights, of boerekos, including braai and potjie. Menus that reflect the mix of culinary cultures that constitute Cape heritage fare can also be found at venues that range from beach bomas to Branewynsdraai restaurant and wine house (below) in Robertson, from cottages in Franschhoek to hilltop spit braais in Durbanville.

Visit the website at www.africandream.org.

ROBERTSON

JEANETTE'S ELAND WITH A SOUR-FIG CONSERVE, PORT AND RED-WINE SAUCE

*Jeanette Bruwer, marketing partner and sister of winemaker Abrie, entertains
a constant stream of visitors at Springfield Estate.
Sour figs are the fruit of species of* Carpobrotus, *thick-leaved members of the mesembryanthemum family,
indigenous to the southwestern Cape. They make an excellent preserve or jam* (suurvykonfyt).

about 2 kg eland (or other venison) fillet
7 ml (1½ tsp) coarse sea salt

MARINADE
olive oil
coarsely ground black pepper
2 cloves garlic, roughly chopped
about 5 ml (1 tsp) finely chopped fresh chilli
2 bay leaves, bruised
4 sprigs fresh rosemary

SAUCE
60 ml (4 tbsp) olive oil
trimmed offcuts of venison
50 ml brandy
125 ml (½ cup) chunky sour fig jam
190 ml (¾ cup) Port
250 ml (1 cup) Springfield dry-red wine
500 ml (2 cups) game or beef stock
250 ml (1 cup) cream

Trim the meat, setting aside any offcuts to use while deglazing the pan. Combine a little olive oil with the remaining marinade ingredients and rub the mixture into the fillet. Cover and leave overnight to marinate. Next morning, turn the meat in the marinade and leave until ready to cook.

Make the sauce. Heat the olive oil, add the offcuts and brown over high heat. Remove the meat and deglaze pan with the brandy. Add the sour-fig jam, Port and red wine and cook over high heat, stirring, for 2 minutes. Add the stock, reduce the temperature and simmer for 20 minutes. Add the cream and cook, stirring, for about 3 minutes, then reduce the temperature and simmer until the sauce thickens to the desired consistency.

To cook the meat, remove the fillet from the marinade at least 5 minutes before cooking, and drain. Rub the sea salt all over the meat. Preheat the oven to 180 °C. Heat a deep, heavy-based ovenproof pan or shallow cast-iron dish, and sear on all sides over high heat. The marinade and salt mixture will form a crust. Transfer the pan to the oven and roast the fillet, uncovered, for 10 minutes. Test with a tip of a sharp knife – the inside should be very rare, the outer meat cooked. Leave the meat to rest for at least 5 minutes before carving in thick slices. Drizzle the sauce over each serving and pass the remaining sauce around.

Serves 6–8

HUNGARIAN-STYLE CHILLED APRICOT SOUP

This is a recipe I developed as a good way to use some of my McGregor apricot harvest.

sunflower oil
1 large onion, peeled and finely chopped
1–2 plump garlic cloves, crushed
5 ml (1 tsp) ground coriander
25 ml (5 tsp) flour
500 ml (2 cups) chopped fresh apricots
(pitted but not peeled), or puréed fresh apricots

300 ml white wine,
  preferably McGregor Co-op Colombard
625 ml (2½ cups) chicken or vegetable stock
sugar to taste
salt and freshly ground white pepper
Hungarian paprika
200 ml sour cream
chopped chives

Heat a little oil, add the onion and garlic and cook gently until the onion has softened but not coloured.
Add the coriander and flour and stir well.
Stir in the apricots and wine, and bring to simmering point. Add the stock and return to a simmer.
Cook slowly for about 15 minutes.
Add the sugar, salt and pepper to taste, then season generously with paprika.
Cool the soup before puréeing in batches. Cool, then chill until ready to serve.
Stir in a little sour cream. Serve the soup in chilled bowls, adding a little more sour cream
to each serving and topping with chopped chives.

Serves 4

ROBERTSON

MARGIE'S TOMATO AND BRINJAL TART

Margie and Barry Phillips run McGregor Country Cottages, a collection of rustic thatched self-catering cottages, several of which are national monuments. Margie often caters for groups, and this is a favourite lunch dish. Tomatoes are a popular cash crop in the Robertson/McGregor area, while brinjals (aubergines or eggplant) are grown in many a back garden. Quantities of the filling will vary according to the diameter and depth of your baking pan or pie plate.

CHEESE PASTRY
200 g cake flour
150 g chilled butter, diced
150 g Cheddar cheese, grated
chopped fresh parsley
salt and pepper
egg white

FILLING
brinjals, sliced, salted and left in a colander to degorge
olive oil
grated Parmesan or Parmesan-type cheese
finely chopped garlic
freshly ground black pepper
torn basil leaves or dried basil to taste
firm ripe tomatoes, sliced
250 ml (1 cup) sour cream
2 eggs, lightly beaten

Preheat the oven to 190 °C.
First make the pastry. Place the flour in a large bowl and rub in the butter with your fingertips
until the mixture resembles fine crumbs. Add the cheese, some parsley and season lightly.
Chill the dough for about an hour before pressing it into a tart pan or pie plate. Brush the base of the pastry
with a little egg white, then prick the base. Bake blind for about 15 minutes, and leave to cool.
Reduce the oven temperature to 180 °C.
To make the filling. rinse the brinjal slices and pat them dry. Brush the slices with olive oil
and grill under a preheated grill, turning once, until they start to soften.
Layer the brinjal slices in the tart case, then sprinkle with cheese and season with garlic, pepper and a little basil.
Follow with a layer of tomato slices, then repeat the layers until these ingredients are used up. Whip the cream
and eggs together, pour carefully over the filling and bake the tart for about 20 minutes, or until set and golden.

Makes 1x 28 cm tart

ROBERTSON

Beauty, simplicity and tranquillity make the weft threads, woven through a warp of history and hospitality: this forms the tapestry of Kannaland, or the Little Karoo. In centuries past, the Khoi chewed the leaves of the ever-present kanna shrub, introducing early settlers to this narcotic, which has lent its name to the region. Those who make the time to visit this special part of the Cape will have no need of an indigenous tranquillizer, as the Klein (Little) Karoo will work its own magic with a titillating mix of temptations.

LITTLE KAROO

ABOVE *The ostrich is still synonomous with Oudtshoorn and the Little Karoo.*

OPPOSITE *A Klein Karoo farm dwarfed by the majestic Swartberg mountains (1); colourful straw characters along the R60 (2); Barrydale (3); a popular lunch stop and farmstall at Barrydale (4).*

Our tour starts at the enchanting village of Montagu, quite literally the gateway to the Little Karoo.

If you enter the town through the Cogman's Kloof tunnel at sunset, a free strobe show of gigantic proportions will greet you as the folded sandstone mountains that envelop the town change from pink to lilac, from blue to purple, in rapid succession.

Montagu boasts fascinating museums and historic homes in four architectural styles. For the energetic, there are well-known hiking trails and rock-climbing sites. The hot-water mineral springs attract the health-conscious and gourmets come to indulge in fortified wines and appetizing fare.

Route 62 meanders through fruit-and-wine country to the pretty town of Barrydale, where farmers and artists live side by side amid glorious gardens and orchards of apricots and plums.

The landscape becomes more rugged on the way to Ladismith, with its signature landmark, the Towerkop, looming above. Legend has it that an angry witch was responsible for splitting this peak, producing the strange cloven dome …

The historic mission stations of Zoar and Amalienstein present a glimpse of unhurried and traditional lifestyles, before the R62 crosses the Huisrivier Pass to enter Calitzdorp, also known as the Port capital of South Africa.

Nestled in the Gamka valley, Calitzdorp is also the fruit bowl of the Klein Karoo, lying halfway between

Port cultivars flourish in the warm Gamka valley arund Calitzdorp where five cellars produce some of the best Cape Port wines – which will have to be renamed soon thanks to EU insistence.

LITTLE KAROO

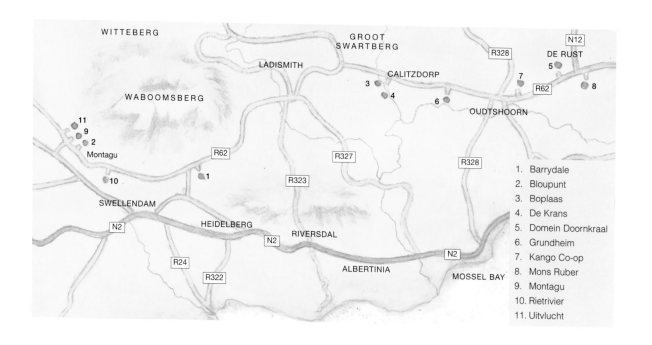

1. Barrydale
2. Bloupunt
3. Boplaas
4. De Krans
5. Domein Doornkraal
6. Grundheim
7. Kango Co-op
8. Mons Ruber
9. Montagu
10. Rietrivier
11. Uitvlucht

Cape Town and Port Elizabeth. The village boasts well-preserved buildings in Karoo styles, most of them with extensive back gardens of orchards and vineyards, set against a backdrop of the formidable Swartberg mountain range.

There are no less than nine mountain passes to explore around Calitzdorp, while the R62 heads through aromatic Karoo scrub to the regional capital of Oudtshoorn, a name synonomous with the Cango Caves and with ostrich farms.

The most easterly point of the Klein Karoo tour – and also of this gastronomic journey through the Western Cape – lies at the beguiling old-world hamlet of De Rust.

What better place to turn back the clock, pour a glass of full-bodied dessert wine and let the space and the silence envelop you.

KLEIN KAROO PRODUCE, FOOD AND RESTAURANTS

Both gourmets and those with simple tastes and hearty appetites are catered for in Kannaland, but the latter undoubtedly have a far wider choice of culinary venues.

Ostrich is the region's most distinctive and most profitable ingredient: it is in demand abroad as it is low in fat, but there is still enough to go around for home consumption too. From the highly prized fillet to the lowly neck, there are cuts to suit every budget. The repertoire of ostrich dishes ranges from gastronomic creations to down-home concoctions, simmering in small black pots.

In Montagu, the number of good restaurants and coffee shops is far greater than the size of the town would seem to warrant. Up there with the best is **Jessica's** in Bath Street, an epicurean heaven where the

menu is contemporary but always includes Karoo specialities such as venison (kudu and springbok) and lamb superbly cooked and sauced.

For something completely different, take a bone-shaking tractor ride to the top of the Langeberg peak for unforgettable views, followed by a potjiekos lunch, on the Burgers' farm.

The Country Pumpkin in Barrydale combines the roles of restaurant, coffee shop and farmstall in style.

Good jams, honey and quality sun-dried tomatoes can be found on the packed shelves.

Deciduous fruit is transformed into delicious preserves in Calitzdorp, and the dried-fruit snacks at **De Krans** cellar make great *padkos* (food for travelling).

No stay in Oudtshoorn is complete without a meal (or three) at the award-winning **Jemima's** restaurant, where traditional Karoo dishes are updated with great flair, and ostrich, naturally, takes pride of place.

Behind its unpretentious exterior, Jessica's fulfils the promise of gourmet expectations.

Sip dessert wines or brandy at Mons Ruber, a historic treasure near De Rust.

WINE, FORTIFIED WINE AND BRANDY

An arid region with very little rain, hot summers and icy winters is not a good prescription for growing and making great wines. That said, the pioneer farmers of Kannaland have been producing dessert wines of good quality – and brandy of varying quality – for more than two centuries.

Today, these fortified products are renowned nationally, while the best of the pot-still brandies are also gracing formal tables in Great Britain.

Meanwhile, contemporary entrepreneurs have discovered small pockets of land – such as Tradouw, near Barrydale – where they are producing some splendid dry table wines. The affordability of the wines increases their appeal.

Montagu is South Africa's Muscadel capital, so that's what you should taste at their three co-operatives – **Montagu, Rietrivier** and **Uitvlucht**. Right in the village is **Bloupunt**, which offers alternatives of Chardonnay and Merlot.

Barrydale Wine Cellar, on the foothills of the Langeberg mountains, is an essential stop on the Little Karoo wine route. The spacious setting allows groups to be accommodated and there's a play area for children.

Allow time to taste some champion wines, notably the Tradouw range, and their excellent five-year-old double-distilled brandy.

Within a stone's throw of each other are **Boplaas** and **De Krans**, two of the five cellars that have put Calitzdorp on the map as the country's Port capital. Both welcome visitors and both produce award-winning Ports in the major styles – ruby, tawny and vintage – along with a range of affordable white and red wines. Boplaas also makes a fine pot-still brandy.

Muscadel and brandies are on the menu at the venerable **Kango Co-operative** in Oudtshoorn, while at **Grundheim**, some way out of town, customers are offered tastes of Muscadels and Ports. But this ostrich-cum-wine farm is best known for its astonishing range of *witblits*, fiery brandy, which is not for the faint-hearted, in spite of their pretty pastel colours and intensely fruity flavours.

In the vicinity of De Rust, **Mons Ruber** estate dreams on, a destination not only for lovers of *soetes* (sweet or dessert wine) and brandy, but a gold mine for amateur historians: This former post house, toll-house and hotel now serves as museum, tasting room and self-catering accommodation offset by green vineyards and scarlet hills.

Off the road to Willowmore, in an isolated mountainous region, lies **Domein Doornkraal**, a farm complex that exhibits impressive self-sufficiency and warm hospitality. Easy-drinking wines for enjoyment rather than contemplation are offered here, epitomised by Tickled Pink, a blush-pink bubbly, slightly sweet, that comes in a bottle decorated with a pink ostrich feather.

MUST-SEE PLACES

Route 62 has been revived, extended and well-marketed. Much of this route is also the old road from Cape Town to Port Elizabeth, a fact that is highlighted on the Route 62 road map, along with a detour from Paarl to Ceres and Tulbagh.

On standard road maps you will find that the R62 appears for the first time on the stretch between Montagu and Barrydale.

Among its many attractions are breathaking scenery, magnificent mountain passes and the absence of traffic. This alternative route to the N2 also encompasses the longest wine route in the world, meandering through the Boland, the Breede River valley and the Little Karoo.

Not only are there at least two coffee shops named after the R62, but at Joubert-Tradouw wine estate outside Barrydale, a blend of Cabernet and Merlot and a Chardonnay both bear this unique name.

For wine lovers, taking the R62 is the only way to do justice to some of the loveliest districts in the Western Cape.

LAMB AND MIXED PEPPER STEW WITH POLENTA CAKES

The walls of Montagu's popular Jessica's restaurant feature doggy prints along with its namesake portrait. Chef-patron Rainer Poewe creates outstanding contemporary fare using quality Little Karoo produce.

1,5–2 kg shoulder of lamb, with bone, cut into pieces
200 ml good-quality olive oil
salt and black pepper
6 large cloves garlic, finely chopped
200 g ham (Parma, Black Forest or pancetta), roughly chopped
a little flour
3–4 medium carrots, peeled and sliced or diced
½ red sweet pepper, seeded and coarsely chopped
½ green sweet pepper, seeded and coarsely chopped
½ yellow sweet pepper, seeded and coarsely chopped
500 g tomatoes, skinned and finely chopped

2 large cloves garlic, peeled but left whole
125 ml (½ cup) coarsely chopped parsley
250 ml (1 cup) dry white wine
400–500 g fresh or frozen peas

POLENTA CAKES
850 ml chicken stock
250 ml (1 heaped cup) polenta
1 large onion, peeled and finely chopped
100 g butter
5 ml (1 tsp) dried mixed herbs

Rub the lamb with a little olive oil, salt and pepper and the finely chopped garlic. Set aside for at least 1 hour. Preheat the oven to 220 °C. Heat the remaining oil in a large pan, and fry the ham for 30 seconds. Transfer to an ovenproof dish. Dust the lamb with flour and brown the pieces in the same oil. Remove and add to the ham. Fry the carrots, peppers and tomatoes in the same oil and add to the lamb. Pound the whole garlic cloves to a smooth paste with the parsley, then add the wine and mix well. Stir this into the lamb mixture and bake for about 1½ hours, stirring every 20 minutes. Add a little more wine if necessary.
Add the peas after 1 hour. Check the seasoning.
To make the polenta cakes, bring the chicken stock to the boil. Add the polenta and boil rapidly for 2 minutes. Reduce the heat to low and cook slowly for 15–20 minutes. Meanwhile, fry the onion in half the butter until golden brown. Add to the polenta, with the mixed herbs, and cook until thick. Transfer the polenta to a pie dish and cut into wedges. Heat the remaining butter in a frying pan and fry the polenta cakes on both sides until golden and crisp. Serve with the lamb.

Serves 4–6

ROASTED NECTARINES WITH CARAMEL SAUCE

Orchards of nectarines, peaches, apricots and plums thrive on farms around Calitzdorp and Barrydale.
This delectable pud would be even more delicious served with homemade vanilla ice cream.

5 firm nectarines, halved, and stones removed
small knob of butter
190 ml (¾ cup) white sugar
125 ml (½ cup) thick cream
5 ml (1 tsp) lemon juice

Preheat the oven to 190 °C.
Place 8 nectarine halves, cut side down, in a
shallow baking dish in a single layer. Roast them,
uncovered, for about 15 minutes until tender.
To make the sauce, dice the two remaining
nectarine halves. Melt a small knob of butter in a
deep frying pan, add the diced nectarines and cook,
stirring, until softened. Remove from the stove and
blend the contents of the pan to make a thick purée.
Heat the sugar in a pan until dissolved, stirring
continuously, then cook it until it turns golden.
Remove from the heat, stir in the cream,
the nectarine purée and the lemon juice.
Serve the nectarine halves topped with
the caramel sauce.

Serves 4

JEMIMA'S CURRIED OSTRICH SOSATIES WITH COCONUT SAUCE

Sisters Annette and Celia le Roux are chef and restaurant manager at Jemima's, the quaint Oudtshoorn restaurant so popular that they seldom get time to go back to the sprawling family farm near De Rust. Annette's cuisine is irresistible and maintains an exquisite balance between gourmet and country, traditional and trendy, as illustrated here with an innovative mix of Cape and oriental.

1 kg ostrich fillet, cut into 3 cm cubes
fresh lemon leaves, bruised
apricot or peach chutney to serve
fresh coriander leaves

MARINADE
500 ml (2 cups) plain yoghurt
10 ml (2 tsp) coriander seeds, roasted and ground, or
10 ml (2 tsp) ready ground coriander
5 ml (1 tsp) cumin seeds, roasted and ground, or
5 ml (1 tsp) ready-ground cumin
1 knob of fresh ginger, peeled and grated (about 50 ml)

30 ml (2 tbsp) peeled and crushed garlic
30 ml (2 tbsp) tomato paste
30 ml (2 tbsp) good-quality apricot jam
30 ml (2 tbsp) freshly squeezed lemon juice
2 green chillies, finely chopped
10 ml (2 tsp) garam masala
30 ml (2 tbsp) sunflower oil

COCONUT SAUCE
125 ml (½ cup) desiccated coconut
400 ml can coconut milk or coconut cream
salt or soy sauce

First make the marinade by combining all the marinade ingredients. Add the ostrich cubes and leave to marinate in a cool place for 2 hours, or up to 24 hours, depending on the toughness of the meat.
Meanwhile, make the sauce. Dry-roast the coconut in a frying pan until golden brown.
Add the coconut milk or cream and bring to a simmer. Add the salt or soy sauce to taste. Set aside.
Thread the meat, alternating with the lemon leaves, onto metal skewers. Grill the sosaties on a flat-top grill, under a preheated grill or over a braai (barbecue) until medium done. As ostrich meat is very lean, do not cook it until it is well done. Sprinkle with salt just before the end of grilling time. Pour the sauce over the sosaties as soon as they are cooked and garnish with fresh coriander leaves. Serve with apricot or peach chutney.

Serves 4–6

NOTE: Wooden skewers may be used, but if you use them, soak them in water for 30 minutes first.

*L*ITTLE KAROO

$\mathcal{S}$WARTLAND

The N7 begins its journey north to Namibia a few kilometres from central Cape Town, skirting the sprawling Table View area, reputed to be the fastest-growing suburb in Africa. Once past the housing developments, the scene gradually becomes rural. A few dairy farms still survive on either side of the motorway, pastures followed by rolling hills of green or gold or khaki, depending on the season.

ABOVE *A cellar door at Twee Jonge Gezellen.*

OPPOSITE *Allesverloren (1); sparkling wine cellar, Twee Jonge Gezellen (2); Twee Jonge Gezellen (3); Tulbagh vineyards (4); Riebeek valley vines at dawn (5).*

It is the wheat, canola, some oats and rye that cover the undulating hills that are most characteristic of the Swartland scene. But if you look alongside the road, and in the folds of the hills, you can see patches of dark renosterbos – the indigenous vegetation that, it is said, caused Jan van Riebeeck to name the region Het Zwarte Land, or 'the black country'.

For part of the way, the cold Atlantic gleams on the left, while the misty peaks of Groot Drakenstein are a constant mauve smudge on the distant right before the road dips to enter Malmesbury.

This is the start of the Swartland Wine Route, and the town has a well-stocked wine information office in the De Bron shopping centre.

Northeast of Malmesbury, the Kasteelberg – a lone mountain and fynbos (indigenous vegetation) paradise – marks the way to the Riebeek valley. Here, a vast plain of rare beauty awaits the traveller, a panorama of vineyards and orchards, wheatfields and olive groves that unfolds during the winding descent from the pass.

There are several hamlets in the valley, but the twin villages of Riebeek Kasteel and Riebeek West are probably the best known. Just four kilometres apart, they have become havens for artists and crafters and popular weekend retreats for city dwellers.

Darling is renowned for its annual wild-flower and orchid shows. This delightful village makes a hospitable base for spring flower tours and visits to unspoiled West Coast beaches, from where the R27, the coastal road, offers an alternative route back to Cape Town.

Although a popular getaway destination, Riebeek Kasteel still exudes rustic charm in a setting of great beauty

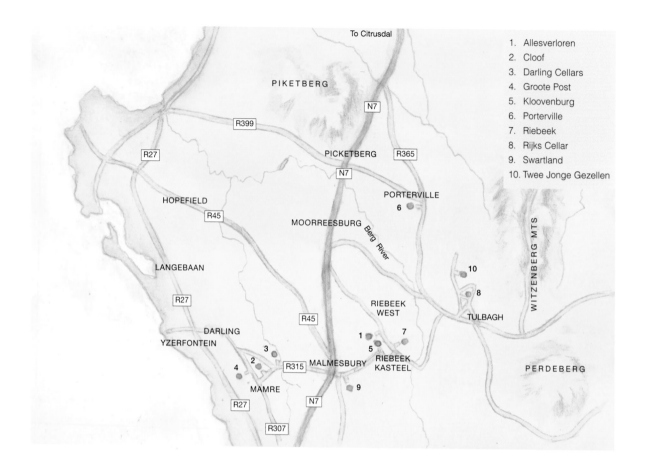

1. Allesverloren
2. Cloof
3. Darling Cellars
4. Groote Post
5. Kloovenburg
6. Porterville
7. Riebeek
8. Rijks Cellar
9. Swartland
10. Twee Jonge Gezellen

THE STAFF OF LIFE – AND MORE
Produce and restaurants

The Swartland's title of 'bread basket of the Cape' is well deserved. Vast quantities of wheat and other grains are harvested and milled in the region, and the giant **Bokomo** group churns out not only cereal and flour, oats and rusks, but it is one of the few producers of dried pasta made from bread flour.

Sugarbird is a venerable Swartland producer of glacé and bottled fruits.

Orchards and fields of protea and fynbos can be found at Op-die-Berg, an enchanting and relatively unknown farming area on a high plateau near Piketberg.

The Riebeek valley offers ideal conditions for peaches and nectarines, and the early varieties are usually first on the Cape market every summer. Recently olive orchards have blossomed across this valley and today table olives and olive oils can be found in village outlets and at a few of the valley wineries, along with farm cheeses.

Former fort and shooting box, the restored cellar lies below the bell tower at Groote Post in the Darling Hills.

In many a dam *waterblommetjies* (Cape pondweed, or *Aponogeton distachyus*) bloom in early spring, giving the lie to those who insist that this species of indigenous hyacinth only grows in the Boland.

The Swartland is also home to several gastronomic entrepreneurs. The **Cape Fruit Vinegar Factory** bottles delectable fat-free dressings in a variety of concentrated fruity flavours, while a Tierfontein farmer transforms his harvest of peppers, chillies and herbs into jams, salsas and pickles under the **Fynbos Fine Foods** label.

Diners looking for traditional Cape fare will find it on the menus of many a small restaurant, along with a side helping of *stampkoring* (crushed wheat) in place of the more usual rice.

Perhaps because of the proximity of the wheatlands, many Swartland cooks pride themselves on their baking

skills, and coffee and tea breaks are often accompanied by heritage treats like buttermilk rusks and syrupy *koeksusters*. Coffee shops open and close, so seek advice from the nearest tourism office as to the best place to find these traditional bakes.

Two venues, both in the Riebeek valley, will interest gourmets. In an unpretentious former stable in Riebeek West, **The Burgundy Snail** delights locals and travellers with contemporary seasonal menus that are good value for money. Advance booking is essential.

Near the village of Hermon, an elegant Victorian farmstead on a large private nature reserve houses **Bartholomeus Klip**, a luxurious country lodge with cuisine to match. Visitors who are not staying over need to book tables in advance.

SWARTLAND WINES

It is no flight of fancy that regional wines make good partners for local fare. Traditionally, Swartland meals were partnered by fruity whites and finished with a palatable port. Today the choice is wide, and local lamb can be accompanied by a number of good red wines.

A visit to **Swartland Cellars**, the big daddy, is a must: This progressive co-op is reaping the benefits of investing in reds, while its whites continue to be popular both locally and in Britain. After sampling the whites, try the Pinotage and the flagship blend, Baron von Imhoff. Swartland is widely regarded as one of the four wineries in South Africa that offer the best value for money among budget-priced wines.

Darling, **Riebeek Kelder** and **Porterville** are co-operative wineries worth visiting. Upgrading and expansion have seen Darling develop into a large, go-ahead operation, offering four labels ranging from quaffable to quality.

Riebeek, previously known for value-for-money whites, today presents both Merlot and Shiraz with some pride.

At Porterville, where large groups are welcome, delicious, easy-drinking wines are sold at bargain prices. They have also produced the first organic wine in the Swartland.

Make time to combine beauty and West Coast history with a visit to **Groote Post**, a magnificent Cape farm in the Darling Hills. Ideally, go in spring, order a picnic, choose one of their agreeable whites and relax on a carpet of flowers. Proceed to **Cloof** (also known as Groene Cloof), which presents interesting reds for tasting.

In the Riebeek valley, sample the Chardonnay at **Kloovenburg**, try the uncommon Tinta Barocca at **Allesverloren** and finish with their port.

THE TULBAGH VALLEY

Tulbagh is often described as the secluded valley, surrounded as it is by no less than three towering mountain ranges. This bewitching village lies just east of the Riebeek valley, and offers diverse attractions in tranquil surroundings. Good food and wine are easy to find, the deciduous fruits are excellent, the historic architecture is appealing, and outdoor sports enthusiasts are spoilt for choice.

Ironically, it was only after the notorious earthquake of 1969 that Tulbagh became renowned for its Cape Dutch architecture; after careful restoration of the 18th-century houses in Church Street, every one of them was declared a national monument.

In one of the oldest houses you will find **Reader's** restaurant, where contemporary country fare is prettily presented. For delicious tastes of traditional Cape cuisine, wander down to **Paddagang**, a regional

Traditional Cape dishes in hearty portions are staples on the menu at Paddagang, Tulbagh's heritage restaurant and regional wine house.

restaurant and wine house on the river's edge. Named after the path taken by the frogs that go a-courting here, these croaking amphibians decorate the labels of light-hearted wines on sale at the restaurant.

More serious tasting sorties should start with **Twee Jonge Gezellen**, a historic estate north of the village, renowned for its flagship bubbly, Krone Borealis Brut. Owner Nicky Krone was first to start night-harvesting in

the Cape, the first to make preservative-free Cap Classique, and was a model employer long before that was in vogue.

Rijk's Private Cellar is part of an attractive guest-house complex. The maiden vintages of both red and white wines have attracted countrywide attention, while at neighbouring **Hunter's Retreat**, the Manley wines are showing great promise.

GINGERED BUTTERNUT SOUP

Butternut soup is always a favourite with South Africans, and there are numerous variations – sometimes simply in the choice of spices, at others with the addition of ingredients such as stock, or apple or orange juice. The Paddagang butternut soup is a rich version, a warming antidote to the icy winds that blow off the snow-capped peaks of Tulbagh's mountain ranges in July. A dry-fleshed pumpkin may be used instead of the butternut squash.

1 kg butternut, peeled and cubed
water to cover
250 ml (1 cup) good-quality chicken stock, preferably homemade
4–5 pieces preserved stem ginger, drained

500 ml (2 cups) cream
15 ml (1 tbsp) brandy
salt and black pepper
additional cream to garnish (optional)
additional pieces of preserved ginger, diced, to garnish

Simmer the cubed butternut in a little water until tender, then drain. Transfer to a food processor or blender, add the chicken stock and ginger pieces and purée the mixture until fairly smooth.

Return the purée to the saucepan and stir in the cream and brandy. Season with salt and pepper, heat to a simmer and cook slowly for about 20 minutes, stirring occasionally.

Serve in warmed bowls, garnished with an additional dollop of cream, if wanted, and sprinkled with a little diced preserved ginger.

Serves 4–5

SUE LONG'S PIZZAS

Sue Long is a food consultant and teacher who is the brain behind the Cape Fruit Vinegar Factory.
Not only is the Swartland a good place to transform flour into pizza bases, but Sue's wonderful fruit dressings
add the finishing touch to cheesy toppings, cutting the richness while adding flavour.
This is her tried-and-trusted recipe, which makes three pizza bases.

BASES
500 ml (2 cups) white bread flour
250 ml (1 cup) brown bread flour
7 ml (1½ tsp) salt
dried herbs (optional)
250 ml (1 cup) skimmed milk
7 ml (1½ tsp) sugar
15 g packet active dried yeast
45 ml (3 tbsp) olive oil
up to 125 ml (½ cup) additional flour, if necessary

TOPPING
home-made tomato sauce
your choice of ingredients, such as sliced
 mushrooms, salami, olives
grated cheese, preferably mozzarella
fresh origanum
Cape Fruit Vinegar, pineapple or lime flavour

First make the bases. Sift the flours and salt into a bowl. Sprinkle in the dried herbs, if using.
Heat the milk to blood temperature, mix in the sugar, sprinkle the yeast on top and leave to prove until frothy.
Stir in the olive oil. Gradually add the yeast mixture to the flours. Knead by hand or with an electric
mixer until the dough is no longer sticky. Add a little extra flour, if necessary.
Place the dough in an oiled bowl, brush the surface with oil and cover with plastic wrap.
Place in a warm spot to rise until doubled in bulk.
Preheat the oven to 220 °C.
Punch down and divide the dough into 3. Roll out each piece of dough and place
on an oiled ovenproof pizza plate.
Add the toppings of your choice, starting with a tomato sauce and finishing with cheese and herbs.
Bake for 15 minutes. Sprinkle generously with pineapple or lime fruit vinegar and serve hot.

Makes 3 pizzas

VANILLA AND YOGHURT
PANNA COTTA WITH QUINCES

*This satiny smooth delight is the creation of Karen Nilsson, restaurateur-chef of The Burgundy Snail
in Riebeek West. Although poached quinces make the ideal partner, other seasonal fruits can be substituted.
Karen suggests pears poached in red wine, strawberries macerated in sparkling wine, or fresh pineapple
tossed in a cherry-based liqueur.*

POACHED QUINCES
2.5 litres (10 cups) water
2 kg castor sugar
2 star anise
1 stick cinnamon
2 whole cloves
6–8 ripe quinces
1 lemon, thickly sliced

PANNA COTTA
500 ml (2 cups) cream
135 g vanilla sugar
15 ml (1 tbsp) gelatine, sponged in a little water
500 ml (2 cups) Greek-style, full-cream yoghurt

Preheat the oven to 150 °C.
To poach the quinces, combine the water, sugar and spices in a heavy-based, ovenproof saucepan,
bring to the boil, then reduce the heat until the syrup is simmering.
Peel and halve the quinces, leaving the cores and seeds intact. Place the quinces and lemon slices in the simmering
liquid, cover with greaseproof paper and a tight-fitting lid. Transfer the saucepan to the oven and poach for
4–5 hours, until the quinces are tender and deep pink. Remove the lemon slices.
If you do not need them immediately, transfer the quinces to sterilized jars and seal.
They will keep for at least 3 months.
To make the panna cotta, combine the cream and vanilla sugar in a small pan. Bring just to the boil,
then remove from the stove and place in a bowl of ice cubes. Stir in the dissolved gelatine mixture. Set aside,
stirring occasionally, until the mixture thickens and cools. Stir in the yoghurt. Divide among 10 small moulds
and refrigerate until set, at least 4 hours.
When ready to serve, unmould the panna cotta on to a flat dessert plate. Top each with wedges of cored
and seeded quince. Drizzle around some quince syrup.

Serves 8–10

Cape
FLAVOUR

OLIFANTS RIVER

Leaving the gentle charms of the Swartland behind us, our journey to the northwest continues, to a long, fertile valley bordered by a unique rock wilderness in the east and lonely stretches of bleached white beaches in the west. If it is spring, much of the landscape will be transformed into a kaleidoscope of colour as wild flowers carpet the region, while the perfume from millions of orange blossoms fills the air in the Olifants River valley.

ABOVE *David Nieuwoudt of Cederberg.*

OPPOSITE *Along with orange groves, visitors will find hot springs, hiking trails and value-for-money wines at Citrusdal.*

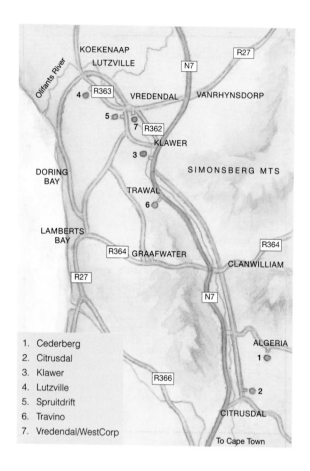

1. Cederberg
2. Citrusdal
3. Klawer
4. Lutzville
5. Spruitdrift
6. Travino
7. Vredendal/WestCorp

The stark beauty and tranquillity of the Cederberg range and its fynbos are celebrated by visitors, hikers, climbers and botanists from all over the world. In the remote Tra-Tra valley, the mission village of Wupperthal offers visitors tastes of traditional fare and sells sturdy *velskoens* (leather shoes) from its thriving shoe factory.

Travellers choosing the N7 will find hot springs and hiking trails at Citrusdal, historic houses and a colourful wild-flower reserve at Clanwilliam. At Klawer, the R362 branches off to Vredendal and Lutzville before reaching the Atlantic Ocean at Papendorp, where it joins the alternative coastal route, the R27.

The coastal resorts are small, unsophisticated and unspoiled. Lamberts Bay is probably the best known, thanks to Bird Island, where visitors can view more than 150 species of bird crowding onto their breeding ground from special platforms.

Along with the seafood and the wine routes, of which more below, travellers can contemplate taking the mission route, through picturesque scenery, or the Van der Stel route which focuses on a few rock shelters used as overnight stops by early travellers along the Copper Way.

HARVESTS FROM OCEAN AND ORCHARD, FIELD AND FARM

Superb seafood, quality vegetables, citrus, deciduous and tropical fruit and game birds can all be found on regional menus. Some cooks stay with time-honoured recipes from the Sandveld and West Coast, mountain and valley, while others transform traditional ingredients into contemporary fare. Both are enhanced by regional wine, and there are a few surprises in store for those in search of traditional food and wine matches …

The red gold of the West Coast is the crayfish, or rock lobster, or *kreef (Jasus lalandii)*, in spite of the fact that

This densely cultivated valley, protected by the mighty Cederberg mountains, presents a striking contrast to the sparsely populated Sandveld, which lies between the Olifants River and the coast.

Elephant feature prominently in open-air galleries of rock art in the region, testimony to the herds that used to roam here. They were still commonplace late in the 17th century, when Dutch explorer Jan Danckaert headed north on what was later to be called the Copper Way, seeking the source of this metal, then used for trade by the Nama people.

today, most of this crustaceous wealth is destined for the export market. It is more affordable at simple seaside eateries, but can be found at inland venues during the prescribed season.

The black mussel can be gathered along rocky shores at low tide, and is also farmed on the West Coast.

Winter is made more acceptable with the arrival of the snoek, along with the northerly gales, while another local traditional delicacy – and something of an acquired taste – is the *bokkom*, or West Coast biltong, as it is also known. Freshly caught harders (mullet) are salted and strung up in bunches to dry in the sun and wind. The results are sometimes served with sultanas as an appetizer to a seafood barbecue, but more generally they are accompanied by buttered brown bread, providing affordable protein for fisher folk.

A wide variety of vegetables is cultivated in the Olifants River valley, while potatoes and sweet potatoes are Sandveld specialities.

Citrus orchards between Citrusdal and Clanwilliam yield the most important harvest in this, the third-largest citrus region in the country. Orange-blossom honey makes a delectable souvenir.

Rooibos tea – rich in minerals and caffeine-free – is another indigenous product that is finding favour among health-conscious consumers across the world. Plantations can be found on the mountainous slopes of the river valley.

The original and most renowned of the West Coast beach bomas, Muisbosskerm, offers rustic seafood feasts and regional specialities.

WINING AND DINING IN THE NORTHWEST

Louis Leipoldt's books on Cape cuisine will make ideal companions to gastronomic exploration in this part of the world. This son of the Cederberg is regarded as South Africa's greatest gourmet and proved to be a prophetic wine connosseur. The annual Cederberg festival, held at Clanwilliam during May, celebrates his contributions, which extend to literature, poetry and medical expertise.

The watery lifeline of the Olifants River enables vineyards to flourish in the dry Klawer area.

It is not difficult to find heritage fare in the north-west. Visitors should not miss out on succulent, well-braaied snoek, partnered by pot bread and *korrelkonfyt* (grape jam with pips). Accompany your fish with a Muscadel from the Olifants River, chilled if the weather is warm. Try a local Chardonnay or an off-dry rosé with black mussels, and reserve the best local white you can find to complement grilled *kreef*.

Beach bomas such as **Muisbosskerm** at Lamberts Bay present seafood feasts on the sands, with a screen of bushes or reeds as protection from the wind. Mussel shells could be the only cutlery available, and the coffee mugs are likely to be made of enamel. Smoked fish or *bokkoms* will probably make the first course, and, along with the freshest fish, potjies simmering over small fires will yield paella-type concoctions, along with meaty *bredies*. The *kreef* will be followed by watermelon or *koeksusters* for dessert.

At **Die Plaaskombuis**, a rustic restaurant south of Lamberts Bay, Tannie Kitta Burger presents traditional Sandveld *boerekos* (country fare). Unhurried breakfasts and teas may be accompanied by nostalgic tales from the past.

Enjoy the casual ambience of the porch at the **Die Voorstrand Restaurant** at Paternoster, and stay with items straight from the sea.

Heading inland, **Strassberger's Hotel** in Clan-william can be relied on for down-to-earth country fare, served with old-fashioned courtesy. The hotel also operates **Reinhold's** restaurant across the road, open for dinner only.

Rustic meals featuring regional fare are served from the **Khoisan Kitchen**, 36 kilometres from Clanwilliam at Travellers' Rest. Except for two months in spring, it opens only if bookings are made for groups of 10 or more.

WEST COAST WINES

The Olifants River farmers have been growing wine grapes for centuries, mainly white varieties that were transformed into quaffable everyday wines, as well as a few good fortified dessert drinks.

Today, the shift towards red wines is also evident here. Some of the best examples are being produced by **Cederberg**, the only estate in the region and the highest cellar in the Western Cape, with vineyards at more than 1 000 metres above sea level.

Citrusdal Cellars can be found near the town of that name, at the foot of the Sneeuberg, where four wine ranges add up to annual production of more than a million bottles. Ivory Creek is the premium brand, Piekenierskloof reds are worth tasting and Goue Vallei offers easy-drinking, budget-priced wines.

Heading north, two cellars where wines are sold at yesterday's prices are **Travino** (formerly Trawal) and **Klawer**.

Spruitdrift still sells bargain-priced unwooded reds and whites under its own label, but its merger with **Vredendal Winery**, the largest and oldest cellar in the valley, has produced a colossus called **WestCorp**.

It can lay claim to being the largest winery under one roof in South Africa, and produces the greatest volume of wine in the southern hemisphere. Although exports form the bulk of their production, groups are welcome and visitors will find accessible, consistent, well-made wines at equally friendly prices. Here, in big sky country, more than 15 per cent of South African wine exported to the UK is produced, with two WestCorp labels coming in among the Top 20 best-selling wines in the UK.

The most northerly Western Cape cellar is **Lutzville Vineyards**, which follows the local pattern of producing a good variety of early-drinking wines at very palatable prices.

SANDVELD PATATS FROM
TANNIE KITTA BURGER OF PLAASKOMBUIS

*Health-conscious cooks can stop reading right here and turn the page – I would not like to be responsible
for the horrified reaction that is likely when the quantity of sugar required for the following recipe is noted.
It is no error, however: it is the generous quantity of sugar that transforms cubed
or sliced sweet potatoes into syrupy golden blocks.
From her farm kitchen, where she cooks traditional* boerekos *on an old coal stove, Tannie Kitta says
(translated from Afrikaans): 'When you talk about sweet potatoes and potatoes, you are talking about real
Sandveld produce …. Sweet potatoes are baked in the oven or covered with hot ashes, and this delicious
anise-flavoured dish is served with roast leg of mutton for Sunday lunch.'
This recipe can easily be halved.*

10 large sweet potatoes
300 g butter or margarine
about 2 kg sugar (correct!)
30 ml (2 tbsp) aniseed
custard powder slaked in a little water

First of all, says Tannie Kitta, peel your sweet potatoes under salted water to stop them turning black.
Put a large wide saucepan over gentle heat and add the butter. While the butter melts, cut the sweet potatoes
into blocks about 2 cm square, returning them to the salted water after cutting.
When the butter has melted, add the drained sweet potatoes and immediately sprinkle with some
of the sugar. Cook slowly, sprinkling more sugar over as that in the pan dissolves. Do not stir.
No water is used in this recipe, and if sugar is not added continuously, the sweet potato will blacken.
Continue cooking until the sweet potatoes are tender, then sprinkle over the aniseed.
If the sweet potato has produced a lot of liquid, thicken it with the custard powder paste.
Shake the pan immediately after adding the paste, but do not stir.

Serves 20 or more, depending on size of potatoes

VENETTE'S DATE PUDDING WITH TOFFEE SAUCE

*Tannie Kitta also sent me this wonderful winter pudding recipe. Fresh dates come from the area
to the north of Lamberts Bay, and rooibos tea is grown in the Cederberg district, around Clanwilliam.*

375 ml (1½ cups) dates, pitted and chopped
300 ml hot rooibos tea
110 g butter
170 g castor sugar
3 eggs
5 ml (1 tsp) bicarbonate of soda
5 ml (1 tsp) vanilla essence
5 ml (1 tsp) instant coffee powder, dissolved
in 10 ml (2 tsp) water

375 ml (1½ cups) self-raising flour
10 ml (2 tsp) salt

TOFFEE SAUCE
60 ml (4 tbsp) brandy
220 g butter
110 g brown sugar
60 ml (4 tbsp) thick cream

Soak the dates in the rooibos tea for about 15 minutes.
Preheat the oven to 180 °C.

Meanwhile, cream the butter and sugar until light and
creamy, then add the eggs, one by one, whisking the mixture after each addition. Add the bicarbonate of soda,
vanilla essence and coffee mixture. Sift the flour and salt,
then fold into the creamed mixture, alternating with the
date mixture. Mix well, then transfer to a buttered ovenproof dish, measuring about 25 x 32 cm, and bake for
about 1½ hours, or until a knife inserted in the centre
comes out clean.

Meanwhile, make the sauce by combining all the
ingredients and heating them over low heat, stirring until
the sugar has dissolved. Bring to boiling point and pour over
the pudding as soon as it comes out of the oven. Prick the
surface of the pudding to allow the sauce to penetrate.

Serves 8

FOOD AND WINE FESTIVALS

This is not meant to be a comprehensive list of Western Cape festivals but it aims to list the events in which food and wine plays a major role and which are more than just commercial affairs held to boost the profits of a single company, farm or manufacturer. Telephone numbers change, tourism policies evolve and even festivals change names and venues, alter their character, and disappear from the map! So it is essential check with the relevant organisations when planning itineraries.

CALITZDORP PORT FESTIVAL

Port, local produce, boules and dominoes are on the menu designed to counter the chill of a Klein Karoo July weekend.
Telephone Calitzdorp Tourism on 044 213 3775 for more information.

CAPE GOURMET FESTIVAL

This is a multifaceted celebration held in May in various venues around Cape Town. Both local and overseas chefs present dinners, demos and workshops, while restaurants put on special menus and the fortnight concludes with the Good Food & Wine Show.
For information, telephone 021 465 0069.

CAPE OLIVE FESTIVAL

This hugely popular event has moved from its original venue at Groot Constantia to the Castle of Good Hope in the city, where it takes place in October.
For more information, telephone Ansie Kamfer on 083 368 8086 or inquire at Cape Town Tourism on telephone 021 426 4260.

CAPE TIMES WATERFRONT WINE FESTIVAL

Another very popular four-day event in May when about 100 of the top Cape wine producers present their wares for tasting in a giant marquee at the Waterfront and small producers also present boutique cheeses and deli items.
For information, telephone 021 408 7632

CRAYFISH & CULTURAL FESTIVAL, LAMBERTS BAY

This is held over a weekend during March and presents a programme of activities ranging from sport to pop concerts, designed to appeal to a wide audience. But seafood-lovers will find *kreef* (crayfish) mussels, snoek and other West Coast fish on the menu. Telephone Lamberts Bay Tourism on 027 432 1000 for more information.

BASTILLE FESTIVAL, FRANSCHHOEK

Held over the weekend closest to 14 July, Franschhoek goes Gallic for a weekend that sees red, white and blue bunting envelop the town, while restaurants present French menus partnered by valley wines and various cultural events add to the range of attractions.
Telephone the Tourism Office on 021 876 3603 for more information.

ELGIN FESTIVAL

This is a well-organised three-day event held in late October or early November that draws the crowds to this farming region. The proceeds go to charity, and the focus is as much on beautiful gardens and roses as on local products, like apples, pears and wine. It is held in the beautiful setting of the Elgin Country Club. Telephone 021 859 3573 for more information.

HERMANUS FOOD & WINE FESTIVAL

In 2003 this was held in August, but this could change in future years. This festival focuses on Overberg wines, locals cheeses and other products of the region, brought together to a venue in the town. Telephone the Hermanus Tourism Office on 028 312 2629 for more information.

KALK BAY HOLY TRINITY CHURCH FISH FARE

This takes place over a March weekend and is a very popular event with both locals and visitors – a wide variety of seafood is cooked and presented in the church gardens. Telephone the church on 021 788 1641 for more information.

MONTAGU MUSCADEL FESTIVAL

This used to be a highlight on the calendar at this pretty town, but then it faded from the scene. It is hoped to revive the event in 2003. Telephone the Tourism Office on 023 614 2471 for more information..

NAPIER PATATFEES

The little Overberg village of Napier is renowned for its quality *borrie patat* or sweet potatoes which are harvested in June. A rural celebration is held in the town where the sweet potato is teamed with snoek for traditional treats and visitors also come to take part in the cycle and running races. Telephone the Tourism Office on 028 423 3325 for more information.

PRINCE ALBERT OLIVE FESTIVAL

Held late April or in May, this historic Karoo village makes a great destination for olive-lovers, although the festival can be a low-key affair. There are a couple of good restaurants and excellent cheese to be discovered as well. Telephone the Tourism Office on 023 541 1366 for more information.

ROBERTSON FOOD & WINE FESTIVAL

This is another appetizing country affair, popular with both locals and city-dwellers who flock to Robertson to attend this celebration and to stock up on valley wines. It is always held in October, usually in the show grounds. Telephone the Tourism Office on 023 626 4437 for more information.

SA NATIONAL CHEESE FESTIVAL

In two short years this four-day event has become hugely popular and deservedly so. Well-organized and publicized, although a little crowded, it is held during April at Bien Donné, a historic fruit and herb farm at Simondium, off the road to Franschhoek. It is an excellent showcase for small producers of farmhouse cheeses from across the country. Telephone Agri-Expo on 021 975 4440 for more information.

SIMONSBERG WINE & FOOD FESTIVAL

The Simonsberg ward of the Stellenbosch wine region organizes a popular December event held about 10 days before Christmas in a farm setting. Excellent local culinary products accompany the superior wines of this beautiful part of the Boland. Telephone 021 888 4615 for more information.

SWARTLAND FOOD & WINE FESTIVAL

Held in June in the 'wheat capital', Malmesbury, this is traditionally a relaxed rural affair, offering appetizing local dishes and affordable wines from stallholders. Telephone the Malmesbury Museum on 022 482 2332 for more information.

V&A WATERFRONT WINTER FOOD FAIR

Although this is a commercial event held in mid-August, it usually offers visitors a varied feast of warming tastes, from new products to chefs demonstrating South African specialities. Telephone 021 556 8200 for more information.

YELLOWTAIL FISH FESTIVAL, STRUISBAAI

Traditionally held in late February when this species is plentiful, guests are invited to land their own catch or watch the locals in action, while they catch and prepare this meaty fish in time-honoured ways. There's a fun run as well. Telephone the Cape Agulhas Tourism office on 028 424 2584 for more information.

GENERAL INDEX

@ the Hills 18, 19, 23
33 Stellenbosch 37, 38
96 Winery Road 46, 47, 49, 51
Agterkliphoogte Co-op 112, 117
Agusta-Grand Provence 74
Allesverloren 136, 137, 140, 142
Alto 49
Altydgedacht 18, 19, 22
Arabela Country Estate 91
Asara 32, 33
Ashanti 59, 60
Ashton 112, 113, 115, 116, 117
Augusta-Grande Provence 76
Avondale 59, 60
Avontuur 49, 50, 105
Backsberg 59, 60, 105
Bains Kloof 104
Barrydale 105, 124–128, 131, 133
Beaumont 86, 87, 90, 92
Berghuis 37
Bergkelder 33
Bergsig 102, 104
Beyerskloof 33, 34
Blaauwklippen 37, 46, 47, 49
Bloemendal 22
Bloupunt 128, 130
Boekenhoutskloof 74, 76
Boland Kelder 59, 60
Bon Courage 110–112, 116, 117
Bonnievale 9, 112, 113, 116, 117
Boplaas 105, 128, 130
Boschendal 70, 71, 74, 75, 76
Bosman's 54, 55, 58
Bot River 88, 90, 92
Bottelary 32
Bouchard-Finlayson 86–90, 93
Bovlei 59, 62
Branewynsdraai 110, 111, 114, 117
Bread & Wine 74
Buitenverwachting 10, 11, 14, 15
Burgundy Snail, The 142
Cabrière 74, 76, 105
Café Petite 15
Café Rosa 114
Caledon 90, 92
Calitzdorp 105, 126–130, 133
Cape Cuisine Route 117

Cape Fruit Vinegar 141, 145
Cape Gourmet Festival 157
Cape Olive Festival 157
Cape Times Waterfront Wine
    Festival 157
Cape Town 9, 12, 30, 157
Castle Wine and Brandy Co. 103
Cathedral Cellar (KWV) 54, 55, 60
Cederberg 149–153
Ceres 100, 104, 131
Chamonix 74, 76
Citrusdal 147, 148, 150, 151, 153
Clanwilliam 150–152, 153, 156
Cloof 140, 142
Clos Malverne 33, 35
Constantia 9, 11–17
Constantia Uitsig 15
Country Pumpkin, The 129
Crayfish & Cultural Festival 157
Darling 9, 140, 141, 142
De Krans 128, 129, 130
De Ou Pastorie 49
De Oude Paarl Wijnhuis 60
De Oude Welgemoed 18, 19, 23
De Rust 9, 92, 105, 128, 130–134
De Trafford Wines 33, 36
De Volkskombuis (Spier) 37
De Wetshof 112, 116
Deetlefs Estate 102, 103–104
Deetlefs, Kobus 104
Delaire 33, 34, 37
Delheim 33, 34
Devon Valley 35, 37, 40
Diemersfontein 59, 62
Dieu Donné 74, 76
Distell 30–31, 33
Domaine Brahms 59, 60
Domein Doornkraal 128, 130
Du Toitskloof 61, 100, 102–104
Duck Pond, The 37
Durbanville 9, 19–27, 117
Durbanville Hills 18, 19, 20–22
Eikendal 49
Elgin 9, 87, 88, 90, 91, 96, 157
Fairview 54, 55, 59, 60
Figaro Restaurant (Spier) 44
food and wine festivals 157–158

Fraai Uitzicht 1798 115
Franschhoek 9, 71–85, 105, 117
Franschhoek Vineyards 74, 76
French Connection, The 74, 80
Genadendal 93
Glen Carlou 59, 60
Good Food & Wine Show 157
Graafwater 150
Graham Beck 110–112, 116, 117
Grande Roche 58
Green Door, The 37
Groot Constantia 10,–14, 157
Groot Drakenstein 72, 138
Groote Post 140, 141, 142
Grundheim 105, 128, 130
Guinea Fowl, The 37
Hamilton Russell 87, 90, 93
Hartenberg 32, 33
Haute Cabrière 74, 75
Hazendal 32, 33, 37
Helderberg 9, 47–53, 128
Hermanus 9, 88, 90, 93, 94, 157
Hermitage, The 37
High Constantia 14
Hildenbrand Estate 59, 62
Hillcrest Berry Orchards 36, 37, 42
Homecraft Centre 21–22
Hopefield 140
Huguenot Fine Chocolates 73
Huguenot Memorial 76
Hunter's Retreat 143
Institute of Culinary Arts (ICA) 40
Jacobsdal 32, 33
JC Le Roux 33, 35, 40
Jemima's 129, 134
Jessica's 128–129, 132
Jonkershoek Valley 35
Jonkershuis (Groot Constantia)
    10, 11, 14, 16
Jonkershuis (Spier) 37
Joostenberg 34, 37
Jordan 31, 32, 33
Joubert-Tradouw 131
Kaapsche Jongens 12, 106
Kaapzicht 32, 33
Kalk Bay Fish Fare 158
Kango Co-op 105, 128, 130

Kanonkop 31, 33, 34
Kanu 32, 33
Karoo Botanical Gardens 100
Kassiesbaai 93
Kasteelberg 138
Khoisan Kitchen 153
Klawer 150, 152, 153
Klein Constantia 10, 11, 14
Klein Oliphantshoek 74, 80
Kloovenburg 140, 142
Kontreikos in die Fynbos 62
KWV 54, 55, 59, 60, 103, 105
L'Avenir 33, 34
L'Ormarins 74, 75, 76
La Colombe 15
La Concorde 54, 55
La Fromagerie 73
La Grange 73
La Motte 70, 71, 74, 76
La Petite Ferme 70, 71, 75, 76
Laborie 54, 55, 59, 60, 105
Lady Phillips 46, 47, 49, 52
Laibach 33, 34
Lake Marais 100
Lamberts Bay 150, 153, 156, 157
Landskroon 59, 60
Lanzerac 28, 29, 33, 35, 37
Le Ballon Rouge 74
Le Bonheur 33, 34
Le Grand Chasseur 112, 117
Le Quartier Français 70, 71, 75,
    76, 84
Lievland 33, 34
Little Karoo 103, 105, 125–135
Lord Neethling Restaurant 28, 29
Louisenhof 37, 105
Lutzville 9, 150, 153
Malmesbury 138, 140, 158
Marine Hotel 90, 91, 94
McGregor 112, 113, 114, 117, 122
Merwida Co-op 102, 104
Middelvlei 33, 35
Môreson 74, 76
Mons Ruber 105, 128, 130, 131
Mont Rochelle 74, 76
Montagu 105, 126–131, 158
Moorreesburg 140

Morgenhof 33, 34, 37
Morgenster 8
Muisbosskerm 151, 153
Muratie 33, 34, 35
museums 13, 37, 49, 76, 90, 93,
    100, 105, 130
Napier Patatfees 158
Nederburg 55, 59, 60
Neethlingshof 28, 29, 32, 33
Neil Ellis 33, 35
Nelson's Creek 59, 60
Newton Johnson 90, 93
Nuy Co-op 98, 99, 100, 102, 104
Nuy Valley Guest House 100
Old Mill Lodge 113, 115
Olifants River 149–156
Opstal 102, 104
Orchard, The 90
Oude Nektar 28, 29
Oudtshoorn 105, 125, 128, 134
Overberg 87–97, 157, 158
Overgaauw 32, 33
Overhex 98, 99, 101
Paarl 9, 55–69, 103, 105, 131
Paarl Vintners 9, 60
Paddagang 142–143, 144
Paul Cluver 90
Pavilion 90–91
Perdeberg Co-op 59, 60

Peregrine 90
Plaaskombuis, Die 153, 154, 156
Plaisir de Merle 74, 76
Pontac Manor 54, 55, 58, 68
Poplar's 6, 7, 18, 19, 23
Porterville 9, 140, 142
Premiere 91
Rawsonville 103, 104
Reader's 142
Reinhold's 153
restaurants 12, 13–15, 21, 23,
    36–37, 49, 60, 61–62,
    73–77, 128–129, 142, 153
Rhebokskloof 56–57, 59, 60, 64
Rickety Bridge 70, 71, 74, 76
Riebeek West 138, 142, 146
Riebeek-Kasteel 138–139
Rietrivier Co-op 128, 130
Rijk's Private Cellar 140, 143
Robertson 9, 104, 111–123, 158
Roodezandt 112, 117
Rooiberg Winery 112, 117
Rose Garden, The 49
Ruitersvlei 59, 60
Rustenberg 31, 33, 34
SA National Cheese Festival 158
Sandveld 150, 153, 154
Saxenburg 32, 33, 37
Seidelberg 58–60

Simonsberg 34, 158
Simonsig 32, 33
Simonsvlei 59, 60
Somerset West 8, 9, 48, 49, 90
Spaanschemat River Café 10, 11, 15
Spier 28, 29, 32, 33, 37
Springfield 112, 116, 117, 118
Spruitdrift 150, 153
Steenberg 13, 15
Stellenbosch 8, 9, 29–45, 103, 105
Stony Brook 74, 76
Sugarbird 140
Swartberg 124, 125, 128, 137–147
Swartland 140, 142, 158
SylvanVale 33, 35
Taphuis Grill, The 37
Thelema Vineyards 31, 33, 34
Three Streams 72–73
Topsi & Co 74
tourism offices 157–158
Towerkop 126
Travino (Trawal) Cellars 150, 153
Tulbagh 9, 131, 136, 137, 140–144
Twee Jonge Gezellen 136, 137,
    140, 143
Uitkyk 33, 34, 105
Uitvlucht Co-op 128, 130
Van Loveren 110, 112, 114–116
Vendôme 59, 60

Vergelegen 46, 47, 49, 52
Vergenoegd 47, 49
Victoria & Alfred Waterfront 157,
    Winter Food Fair 158
Vignerons de Franschhoek 9, 76
Villiera 33, 34
Vlottenburg 32, 33, 105
Voorstrand Restaurant, Die 153
Vredendal Winery 150, 153
Waboomsrivier 102, 104
Walker Bay 88, 91–91, 93
Walker Bay Wines 6, 7, 86, 87
Wamakersvallei Winery 59, 62
Waterford 6, 7, 30–31, 33, 36
Wellington 9, 55–69, 103
Weltevrede 112, 116
West Coast 23, 142, 150–151
WestCorp 150, 153
Western Cape Hotel and Spa 91
Windmeul Co-op 59, 60
Wine & Company 93
Wine magazine 32
Wolseley 102, 104
Worcester 9, 99–109
Yellowtail Fish Festival 158
Zandvliet 112, 116, 117
Zandwijk 59, 60
Zevenwacht 28, 29, 32, 33
Zlomke, Frank 58

RECIPE INDEX

**SOUPS, STARTERS,
SALADS & SIDE DISHES**
Chicken salad with fruit and nuts 38
De Oude Welgemoed's mushroom
    and blue cheese mousseline 24
Duncan's smoked salmon fish tea 78
French Connection's smoked duck salad
    with a raspberry verjuice dressing 80
Gingered butternut soup 144
Gorgonzola custard with pickled fennel
    and tomato confit 84
Hungarian-style chilled apricot soup 120
Lady Phillips smoked salmon on blinis 52
Marinated goat's-milk cheese 63
Sandveld patats from Tannie Kitta Burger
    of Plaaskombuis 154
Spaanschemat River Café prawn and grape-
    fruit salad with mango dressing 17
ICA waterblommetjie and anchovy gratin
    with sparkling wine 40

MAIN COURSES
Bacon-wrapped sirloin with black
    mushrooms and a red-wine glaze 26
Chicken with tomato jam 51
Duo of yellowtail and tiger prawns
    with mascapone and warm bean
    sprout salad 94
Jeanette's eland with a sour-fig conserve,
    Port and red-wine sauce 118
Jemima's curried ostrich sosaties with
    coconut sauce 134
Jonkershuis smoorsnoek 16
Lamb and mixed pepper stew with polenta 132
Margie's tomato and brinjal tart 122
Pontac Manor's flambéed lamb kidneys 68
Rhebokskloof smoked ostrich fillet with
    goat's-milk chhese and olive mousse 64
Sue Long's pizzas 145
Vegetable panini 50
Wellington lamb knuckle with dried fruit 66

DESSERTS & CAKES
Brandy truffles 107
Decadent chocolate cake 44
Elgin Farmstall special apple cake 96
Hillcrest Berry Orchards raspberry
    muffins 42
Honey lavender ice cream with dainty
    biscuits 82
Kaapsche Jongens 106
Malva pudding 108
Roasted nectarines with caramel
    sauce 133
Vanilla and yoghurt panna cotta
    with quinces 146
Venette's date pudding with
    toffee sauce 156